Ask, Thank, Tell

Improving Stewardship Ministry
in Your Congregation

Charles R. Lane

D1015349

Augsburg Fortress
MINNEAPOLIS

ASK, THANK, TELL
Improving Stewardship Ministry in Your Congregation

Large-quantity purchases or custom editions of this book are available at a discount from the publisher. For more information, contact the sales department at Augsburg Fortress, Publishers, 1-800-328-4648, or write to: Sales Director, Augsburg Fortress, Publishers, P. O. Box 1209, Minneapolis, MN 55440-1209.

Scripture passages are from the New Revised Standard Version of the Bible, copyright © 1946, 1952, 1971, 1989 by the Division of Christian Education of the National Council of the Churches of Christ in the USA. Used by permission.

Library of Congress Cataloging-in-Publication Data
Lane, Charles R., 1948-
  Ask, thank, tell : improving stewardship ministry in your congregation / Charles R. Lane.
     p. cm.
  Includes bibliographical references.
  ISBN 0-8066-5263-2 (pbk. : alk. paper)
  1. Stewardship, Christian. I. Title.
  BV772.L34 2006
  248'.6—dc22   2005032008

Cover design by Laurie Ingram; Cover photo © age fotostock / SuperStock. Used by permission.
Book design by Michelle L. N. Cook

The paper used in this publication meets the minimum requirements of American National Standard for Information Sciences—Permanence of Paper for Printed Library Materials, ANSI Z329.48-1984. ♾ ™

Manufactured in the U.S.A.

10   09   08   8   9   10

Contents

Preface

THIS BOOK GROWS OUT OF MY AFFECTION FOR GOD'S PEOPLE
gathered in congregations. The background and the insights I
share grow from serving three different Lutheran congregations
over twenty-one years, working with hundreds of congregations while on the staff of the Northwestern Minnesota Synod
of the ELCA for nine years, and now serving congregations as
an ELCA churchwide staff member.

I have seen too many congregations denied the joy of giving by a mentality that sees stewardship only as a way to get the
congregation's bills paid. Not surprisingly, in these congregations, serving on the stewardship committee is viewed as a duty
to be endured by the poor souls who draw the short straw. I
have seen other congregations where giving is understood to be
an important part of each person's faithful response to a loving
God. Not surprisingly, in these congregations, serving on the
stewardship committee is viewed much more positively.

My hope in writing this book is to provide a way for all
congregations to move to a healthier place, a place where stewardship is grounded in God's Word, not simply in the needs of

the congregation; a place where giving is an act of discipleship, not a duty of membership; a place where money is talked about openly and honestly; a place where faithful giving is an important part of faithful lives.

I could fill this book with words of thanks and still leave someone out. I thank God for my colleagues and the people of St. Mark Lutheran in Butler, Pennsylvania, St. Philip's Lutheran in Fridley, Minnesota, Immanuel Lutheran in Wadena, Minnesota, the Northwestern Minnesota Synod of the ELCA, and now the stewardship team of the ELCA.

I thank God especially for family—for my parents, Ron and Maxine Lane, whose love was unconditional and whose faith was contagious; for my children, Jason and Marta, who bring joy to my heart every time I think of them; and for my wife, Chris, to whom I dedicate this book. Our love brings such incredible joy to our lives that sometimes I just shake my head in wonder.

Introduction

STEWARDSHIP HAS BEEN KIDNAPPED AND IS BEING HELD hostage by a sinister villain named "Paying the Bills."

In too many congregations in our land, the goal of asking people to give to the church is to get enough money to pay the church's bills for the coming year. When people are asked to give to the congregation, they are told of budget crunches, rising costs, and the need to dig a little deeper. At the end of the year, if all the bills are paid, someone will likely say, "Stewardship was good last year." If this sounds like your congregation, stewardship has been kidnapped right out from under your nose.

The goal of this book is to perform a dramatic rescue of stewardship, freeing it from any connection whatsoever to "Paying the Bills." The Bible talks a lot about stewardship, and it talks very little about the need for an institution to get its bills paid. Rather, when the Bible talks about stewardship it almost always talks about the intimate connection between how a person handles financial matters and that person's relationship with God. In the Bible, all stewardship, including financial stewardship, is an intensely spiritual matter. It lies close to the heart of a disciple's relationship with Jesus.

On the pages that follow, I have three goals that can help perform this dramatic rescue.

○ I want to make the case, the biblical case, that stewardship really is all about discipleship. The focus of biblical stewardship is not on the congregation's needs at all. Rather, the focus of biblical stewardship is on the fact that generous giving is one of the basic acts of discipleship. If stewardship is to be rescued, then the focus must be on the disciple, on the giver, not on the congregation.

○ I want to describe a congregational stewardship ministry that can accomplish the rescue. This stewardship ministry is centered on three simple verbs—ask, thank, and tell. Your congregation's stewardship leaders can come back to these three foundational verbs over and over again, as you help God's people use good financial stewardship to grow closer to God.

○ I want to suggest a structure for your stewardship leadership team that is also based on these three verbs. I want to encourage you to have as few stewardship committee meetings as possible, and instead free stewardship leaders to do stewardship ministry rather than meet about stewardship ministry. Can you create three stewardship teams, one focusing on each verb? Can you turn creative people loose to find new and effective ways to ask, thank, and tell so that God's people might experience joy in giving generously?

If stewardship has been kidnapped from your congregation and replaced by "Paying the Bills," and if your stewardship leaders are committed to performing a rescue operation, I wish you God's blessings on your work. The rescue will not be accomplished overnight. "Paying the Bills" will try over and over again to re-kidnap stewardship. Your work will not be easy. But know that your work is important. I am convinced that there is little in life today that can help a disciple grow in relationship with Jesus more than good, solid, intentional biblical stewardship. You will be doing a huge spiritual favor for God's people who gather in your congregation if you not only accomplish the rescue, but diligently stand guard to keep "Paying the Bills" far, far away, and keep biblical stewardship at the heart of your congregation's ministry.

Chapter 1

Discipleship, Not Membership

WHAT IS THE MISSION STATEMENT OF YOUR CONGREGATION'S stewardship ministry? As your Stewardship Committee gathers to do its work, at what goal are you aiming? Let me suggest a goal for you to consider:

> The goal of our stewardship ministry is to help God's people grow in their relationship with Jesus through the use of the time, talents, and finances God has entrusted to them.

If your congregation is like many congregations, this goal hasn't exactly been on the front burner as you have thought together about stewardship. My hunch is that most congregations haven't thought about a Stewardship Mission Statement, but, based on how they function, it would be something like:

> The goal of our stewardship ministry is to raise enough money to pay the bills next year.

I hope you see the difference. The first goal focuses on the individual giver's relationship with Jesus. It understands that the way the individual uses his or her time, talents, and treasure has a huge impact on their relationship with Jesus. The second goal focuses on the institution, on the congregation, and its needs. The magnitude of this difference cannot be overstated.

Stewardship ministry deserves to have its place alongside all the other ministries of your congregation—and all of them need to focus on making new disciples and helping those actively following Jesus to grow in the relationship that already exists. For too long most of the congregation's ministry has been considered "spiritual," while stewardship ministry has been considered "business." Jesus didn't see it this way, and neither should we.

Let me say it as clearly as I can: Your congregation's stewardship ministry is first and foremost about making and growing disciples. You need to be about the business of helping God's people grow in their relationship with their Lord and Savior Jesus Christ. When this is the primary goal of your stewardship ministry, having enough money to pay the bills will not be a problem.

Discipleship Versus Membership

To see what a difference it makes to focus on the individual's relationship with Jesus rather than on the congregation, we need to think about the difference between discipleship and membership.

A number of years ago I had the privilege of going on a mission trip to India. On that trip, I had a conversation with church leaders from the Andhra Evangelical Lutheran Church. After we had talked for over an hour, the president of the Andhra church said, "This has been a wonderful conversation. Before we began to talk, I believed that the church in the United States was more like a club to which people belonged. Now I have come to see that I have been wrong." His words have haunted me, because I have seen too much evidence in my own life and in the lives of many others that indicates that his first impression might have been all too close to the truth.

In the church that I have grown up in and served as pastor of for almost thirty years, I am convinced that, for most people, the primary relationship is with the congregation rather than with Jesus Christ. When asked about their faith, most people I know will talk first about what is going on in their congregation and only later, if at all, will they describe what is going on in their relationship with Jesus. Most of us are far more inclined to talk about the activities of our congregation than we are to talk about how Jesus is active in our lives. The dominant church paradigm continues to be membership, not discipleship.

Let me describe *membership*. There are certain things that members in a congregation are expected to do. Among these are:

1. Give money to support others who do ministry. Ministry is done by professionals—people like the pastor, a missionary, or those engaged in social service. Members give to pay these professionals.

2. Maintain the institution. Members are expected to give enough money to keep the building heated, lit, and maintained, and to make sure that enough people take their turn on committees and council. It is also important that Sunday school is taught and the youth group led.

3. Live an upright life and be a good citizen. It is important, and expected, that members of congregations contribute to the larger good in the community and don't become public scandals.

There are some assumptions that undergird this paradigm of membership. These include:

1. The mission field is elsewhere. There is a mission field where people are actually moving from unbelief to faith in Jesus Christ. This is an exciting place, and we want to support the work of those who are involved there. However, this mission field is far from where we live.

2. The goal of the congregation is to get and keep members. In many congregations in our country the death rate far exceeds the birth rate. Therefore, it is important to add members to the rolls, and keep them there.

3. Congregations have low expectations of members. The reason for this is obvious: If we expect too much of members, people probably won't join, and if they do join, they won't hang around for long.

Discipleship contrasts sharply with membership. When we talk about discipleship, the primary relationship is not with the congregation. The primary relationship is with Jesus. The congregation is the community of people with whom this relationship is lived out and nurtured. The congregation is not the end. The congregation is the means to the end. In the congregation we grow in faith and proclaim the good news to those who are not hearing that good news on a regular basis.

The role of a disciple, then, is to grow deeper in Jesus and to tell others about Jesus. As a disciple lives his or her relationship with Jesus in a congregation, the disciple understands his or her work to include:

1. Doing the ministry. Disciples don't think the congregation "pays the pastor" to do things. Rather, ministry is a partnership. Instead of complaining about what the pastor isn't doing, disciples understand that ministry belongs to all God's people.

2. Giving as a part of a growing relationship with Jesus. Many lists describe the basic tasks of discipleship. One helpful list is found in Michael Foss' book, *Real faith for Real Life* (Minneapolis: Augsburg Books, 2004). He identifies the following marks of discipleship:

    - Daily prayer,
    - Daily scripture reading,
    - Weekly worship,
    - Growth in giving to the tithe or beyond,
    - Serving others in Jesus' name,
    - Sharing the faith story with the unchurched.

    Along with all the other marks of discipleship, giving is an important part of being in relationship with Jesus and growing in relationship with Jesus.

3. Living life in community. The larger community is the congregation. In many cases a smaller community is a small group that gathers for prayer, study, and service.

    There are also some assumptions inherent in a life of discipleship.

1. The mission field starts at the front door of the church. If America ever was a Christian nation, it certainly isn't any more. In many communities one-third to one-half of the people aren't associated with any Christian congregation. In some areas of the country, the percentage is even higher. Furthermore, two-thirds of those who are associated with a congregation aren't in worship on any given Sunday. There is mission work to do at the front door of the church. (Dare we say there is quite a bit of mission work to do even inside the sanctuary?)

2. The goal is to make disciples for Jesus Christ. It's not that membership in a congregation is a bad thing; it just isn't enough. Disciples are self-consciously in a relationship with Jesus Christ and are more eager to talk about that relationship than about the programs of the church.

3. There are high expectations of disciples. The six traits of discipleship listed above are understood to describe the life of followers of Jesus, and the expectation is that all disciples will be diligent in their practice of these.

By now you may be saying, "Hey, wait a minute. I thought we were talking about stewardship. All of a sudden you've launched into an abstract discussion of membership and discipleship." I reply by saying that this abstract discussion is important for two reasons.

⌒ First, if your stewardship ministry is going to focus on helping people grow in their relationship with Jesus rather than meeting the needs of the congregation, it is very important for your stewardship leaders to stop and think about the nature of your congregation. Does your congregation sound more like the description of membership or the description of discipleship? If the description of membership rings truer to your congregation, then you need to realize that you are going to be breaking some new ground. That's okay. In fact, it's great, because it is ground that needs to be broken, and there's no one better to take the lead than the stewardship folks.

⌒ Second, this discussion is also important because it points to the central place that giving has in whether one sees himself or herself as a member or a disciple. If a believer gives to the institution so that others can do ministry and the congregation can keep going, then that person has a major roadblock in the way of a stronger relationship with Jesus. On the other hand, if that same believer can begin to understand that giving is an act of faith, growing out of a relationship with Jesus, and if that giving can grow toward the tithe, then that believer has taken a huge step toward having stewardship at the heart of his or her relationship with Jesus.

I'm a Lutheran. As such I have a lifetime of conditioning to be nervous about any statement of what God wants us to do. We Lutherans are so nervous about slipping into works of righteousness that we are way too quiet about discipleship. The New Testament makes it perfectly clear that Jesus didn't die on the cross just so we might assent to faith statements and join a congregation, as important as those things are. Jesus died on the cross so that we might be disciples and make disciples. If you have any doubt about the truth of this, look at the end of Matthew's Gospel or at the beginning of Acts.

The conviction of this book is that we are called to be disciples. Furthermore, I am convinced that how we steward the time, talent, and particularly the finances that God has entrusted to us will have a huge impact on our discipleship. In a unique way, financial stewardship has the potential to be either a roadblock to discipleship or a catalyst to a growing discipleship.

Focus on God's Word

In order for the focus of our stewardship ministry to be the believer's relationship with Jesus, God's word must be at the center of all that we do. God's word belongs at the center of our stewardship ministry every bit as much as it belongs at the center of preaching, teaching, and everything else we do together in God's family. Jesus spent a lot of time talking about money and possessions. In the Gospels, Jesus talks more about money and possessions than any other topic except the kingdom of God. There is plenty of material in God's word that can help stewardship be a growing edge for your relationship with Jesus.

In spite of this, congregations have often attempted to fund their ministry by focusing on the budget. When it comes time to talk about financial support for the congregation's ministry, too often next year's budget is paraded before the congregation, and people are asked to increase their giving so that the budget can go up. This is membership giving, not discipleship giving.

Why does this happen? It happens, I think, because often people who are stewardship leaders in congregations are comfortable with budgets and lots of numbers. Often those selected to work with financial matters in the congregation are people who deal with financial matters in their work. Such people are around numbers and budgets all the time. They are comfortable with numbers and budgets. They are even motivated by numbers and budgets.

Most people in our congregations aren't like these financial leaders. Most people in our congregations find their eyes glazing over and their attention span shortening when they look at a page filled with columns comparing this year's numbers to last year's numbers to next year's numbers. They are lost or bored or confused. They are certainly not motivated.

God's word, on the other hand, can and does touch the hearts of God's children. This is, of course, a faith statement. God's word will work in people's lives far more powerfully than any budget. God's word has the power to transform people's lives, even that part of their lives dealing with money and possessions.

As you do stewardship ministry in your congregation, make sure your focus is always on God's word. Find those many and powerful passages in the Gospels in which Jesus talks about the threats and the opportunities that money places before us. Look through the letters of the New Testament and see how the early church handled financial matters. Search the Old Testament and find there the powerful proclamation of God's ownership of all that is, and the other cornerstones for Jesus' teaching.

As you do stewardship ministry in your congregation, make certain God's word is front and center. Pull the budget out for the annual meeting if you must, but don't let it anywhere near your stewardship ministry.

Ask the Right Question

How well I can remember one of my seminary professors, Paul Sonnack, telling his classes over and over again the importance of asking the right questions. He would say, "It is far more important to ask the right question than it is to get the right answer. If you ask the wrong question, the answer doesn't matter. If you ask the right question, even if you get the answer wrong the first time, you still have a chance."

The questions we ask shape the way we think. When it comes to stewardship, the questions God's people ask shape the way they think about money and possessions.

Let's imagine two people sitting in the pew on Sunday morning, filling out their commitment card for their financial support of the congregation for the coming year. Joe is sitting there thinking, "How much of my money does the church need this year? How do I feel about how things are going at church these days? Times are tight, so can I really spare any more?" Next to Joe is Sue. Sue is thinking, "God has blessed me in so many ways. How do I feel God is calling me to respond to those blessings?"

Joe and Sue may be caricatures, but their respective questions speak volumes about how they are thinking. Joe's focus is on the need of the church to receive. Sue's focus is on the need of the giver to give. Joe is giving as a member, thinking first about the need of the institution. Sue is giving as a disciple, thinking first about God's presence in her life and God's call to her to respond to that presence.

As stewardship leaders, one of your goals needs to be to help people ask the right question. As you do your work, find ways to use God's word to help people in the congregation reflect on God's presence in their lives, and then ask, "How is God calling me to respond to that presence?" Find ways to use God's word to help people honestly reflect on all the blessings that have been showered upon them, and then ask, "How is God calling me to use those blessings?"

Summary

The goal of our stewardship ministry is to help God's people grow in their relationship with Jesus through the use of the time, talents, and finances God has entrusted to them.

It is possible to summarize this first chapter by using the well-known stewardship phrase, "Focus on the giver's need to give, not on the church's need to receive."

- ⌒ When we focus on the giver's need to give, we will help God's people grow in their relationship with Jesus through their use of the time, talents, and finances that God has entrusted to them.
- ⌒ When we focus on the giver's need to give, we will inevitably use the language of discipleship, not the language of membership.
- ⌒ When we focus on the giver's need to give, we will find in God's word an invaluable wealth of resources to enrich our understanding.
- ⌒ When we focus on the giver's need to give, we will also help people ask the right question. Don't ask the membership question, "How much does the church need?" Rather, ask the discipleship question, "How is God calling me to respond to God's presence in my life?"

Chapter 2

It All Belongs to God

SEVERAL YEARS AGO I WAS PREACHING TO A GROUP OF PASTORS
at a retreat. In the sermon, I repeatedly referred to the countless
gifts we have received from our loving God. I remember being
very careful to use the word *gifts* to make sure there was no con-
fusion about the fact that we live by the gracious hand of God,
not from our own accomplishments.

Later in the retreat I was in conversation with Pastor Harry
Wendt, president of Crossways International. Harry was one of
the speakers at the retreat. In his gentle, direct way, Harry suggested that I should be careful about using the word *gift.* He
said that God doesn't give gifts, at least not in the way we use
the word *gift.*

He went on to point out that when we use the word *gift*
we imply that one person has given something to someone
else, who then owns that item and is free to do with it as
they please. He concluded his observation by saying that this
is not the way it is with God and us. God continues to own
everything.

Of course, Harry was correct.

When we give a gift to someone, we understand that a transfer of ownership has occurred. Imagine that I buy a gift for my son. After I buy that gift, it belongs to me. I have paid for it. It is mine. Then on a birthday or at Christmas, I wrap that gift (or more accurately, my wife does), and give it to him. He unwraps it, thanks me for the gift, and at that point, it belongs to him. I have given up any claim to it. What he does with the gift from that point on is not in my control; it is in his control. He probably will choose to use his possession in a responsible way, both because he doesn't want to destroy it, and because he doesn't want to disappoint me. However, he is not bound in any way to do this. The gift is his. He owns it.

This isn't the way it is with God and us. No such transfer of ownership occurs. God has created all that is, and God continues to own all that is. Everything we have still belongs to God. We are given the privilege and responsibility to care for that which belongs to our heavenly Father.

This biblical truth—that it all belongs to God—is the cornerstone of everything we have to say about stewardship. The very word *steward* describes someone who watches over that which belongs to someone else. We will talk more about this later in this chapter, but first, let's consider a few passages from Scripture that help us understand this foundational truth.

Psalm 24:1-3

> The earth is the Lord's and all that is in it,
> the world, and those who live in it;
> for he has founded it on the seas,
> and established it on the rivers.

The opening verses of Psalm 24 are a clear and powerful statement of ownership. God owns the earth and all that is in it. The basis for this claim of ownership lies in God's creative act.

God made the world and all that is in it, and therefore owns the world and all that is in it.

We need to recognize the radical nature of this claim. The language that we use every day speaks a different message than the message of the psalmist. We look at a house and we ask, "Who owns that house?" We see a new car parked in a driveway and we ask, "Whose car is that?" When someone buys a new house and takes out a mortgage, he or she will often joke, "The bank and I own this house."

I'm not suggesting that we need to change our language. I am suggesting that we need to recognize that the language we use is very important because it shapes the way we think. The language we use leads us to believe that we are the ultimate owners of the things that are in our control. The world in which we live functions on the assumption that we own the things that are "ours."

The psalmist says, "No. God made it all and God owns it all." This radical claim is the starting point of all the Bible has to say about the world in which we live.

Deuteronomy 8:11-18

Take care that you do not forget the Lord your God, by failing to keep his commandments, his ordinances, and his statutes, which I am commanding you today. When you have eaten your fill and have built fine houses and live in them, and when your herds and flocks have multiplied, and your silver and gold is multiplied, and all that you have is multiplied, then do not exalt yourself, forgetting the Lord your God, who brought you out of the land of Egypt, out of the house of slavery, who led you through the great and terrible wilderness, an arid wasteland with poisonous snakes and scorpions. He made water flow for you from flint rock, and fed you in the wilderness with manna that your ancestors did not know, to humble you and to test you, and in the end to do you good. Do not say to yourself, "My power and the might of my own hand have gotten me this wealth." But remember the Lord your God, for it is he who gives you power to get wealth, so that he may confirm his covenant that he swore to your ancestors, as he is doing today.

The setting of these words from Deuteronomy is very important. Moses speaks them to God's people as they are ready to enter the promised land. They are across the Jordan River, in the present-day country of Jordan. These words are spoken to help them make sense of what is about to happen to them.

These particular verses address a problem that was hardly unique to those forty-year wanderers. When things go well for us, it is very tempting to take credit for them. Of course, when things don't go well, it seems to be human nature to blame someone else. But when things do go well, we want the credit.

This passage from Deuteronomy is especially important for us today, for it describes the accumulation of wealth and the temptation to take credit for all our material successes. Just as the opening verses of Psalm 24 debunk the myth that we are the owners of the things we have, so these verses from Deuteronomy 8 debunk the myth that we are the source of our own wealth. "Do not say to yourself, 'My power and the might of my own hand have gotten me this wealth.' But remember the Lord your God, for it is he who gives you power to get wealth, so that he may confirm his covenant that he swore to your ancestors, as he is doing today" (verses 17-18).

God did not just create the world and all that is in it, and then turn us loose, allowing us to rely on our own craft and creativity. This world isn't about the survival of the fittest. This world isn't a setting for the smartest and the most tenacious to amass the most wealth because of their superior abilities, and then to smugly crow about their accomplishments.

God did not just create the world and turn us loose. God is not only the creator of all that is, God is the source of the wisdom and tenacity. "It is God who gives you power to get wealth." If I have brains that allow me to earn a living, God is the source of those brains. If I have strength that allows me to earn a living, God is the source of that strength. If I am fortunate enough to live in a country that is flowing with milk and honey, and has wealth beyond that enjoyed by any country in all of history—God is the source of that as well.

Since God is the owner of all that is, and since God is the source of all the abilities and resources that allow me to live a more than comfortable life, then there is no room left for me to imagine that I am the source of my good life. God is.

The proper response to the blessings of this life is not to pat myself on the back and try to find a way to get more stuff. The proper response is to give God the glory and the thanks and to ask serious questions about how I am called to use what God has entrusted to me.

Genesis 1:27-28

> So God created humankind in his image, in the image of God he created them; male and female he created them. God blessed them, and God said to them, "Be fruitful and multiply, and fill the earth and subdue it; and have dominion over the fish of the sea and over the birds of the air and over every living thing that moves upon the earth."

There has been much debate for centuries over the meaning of the word *dominion,* but this much is clear:

- ◯ Humanity has the highest place in the created order.
- ◯ A delegation of authority occurs here. God the creator transfers some authority over the creation to human beings.
- ◯ There is not a transfer of ownership. God the creator is still God the owner.

Humanity has the highest place in the created order. Psalm 8:3-5 says it best:

> When I look at your heavens, the work of your fingers,
>> the moon and the stars that you have established;
> what are human beings that you are mindful of them,
>> mortals that you care for them?
> Yet you have made them a little lower than God,
>> and crowned them with glory and honor.

In all the majesty of God's creation, men and women have been given the highest place. Along with the psalmist we may marvel that this is so, but clearly it is. Part of the created order is the primacy of humanity.

A delegation of authority occurs here. Again, from Psalm 8, now verse 6:

> You have given them dominion over the works of your hands;
>> you have put all things under their feet.

Just as the CEO of a company delegates authority in some areas to other employees, God has delegated authority to humanity. People have dominion over the created order, and this is the way God has intended it to be from the beginning.

There is not a transfer of ownership. Humanity has the highest place in the created order, but we are still part of the created order. We are accountable to God for how we exercise our dominion. A very clear example of this comes just two chapters after humans are given dominion. In Genesis 3 we find the man and the woman exercising their dominion in violation of the instructions of the creator. They eat from the forbidden tree, and as a result not only is hardship brought into their lives, but they are also banished from the garden. God still owns what

God has created, and dominion must be exercised in accordance with God's direction, or there will be negative consequences.

Steward

Having considered these passages from the Old Testament, it is time to take a look at the word *steward*. The word *steward* most likely comes from two old English words that named the person who cared for the pigs of another. This person was called the sty-warden. This is helpful to remember, for the original situation of the word tells us two very important things. First, the sty-warden didn't own the pigs. Second, the sty-warden cared for the pigs.

Looking more specifically at the Old Testament, we can say three things about the steward. First, the steward is not the owner (are you getting sick of hearing that yet?). Second, the steward has a position of high authority in the household of the owner and is given great responsibility. Third, the steward cares for the possessions of the owner both for the benefit of the owner and for the benefit of other people who depend on the owner for their well being.

I don't want to belabor the point, but it needs to be said. The steward is not the owner. The steward is always one who cares for that which belongs to another. There are no exceptions to this statement.

The steward has a position of high authority in the household of the owner and is given great responsibility. Genesis 43 and 44 tell the story of the sons of Jacob visiting their brother Joseph in Egypt. It is very interesting to read these chapters with an eye on the role of the steward in Joseph's house. The steward obviously sits close to the side of Joseph, is the most important and most trusted of the servants, and is given important instructions with the assumption that they will be carried out precisely as the owner has directed.

The steward cares for the possessions of the owner, both for the benefit of the owner and for the benefit of other people who depend on the owner for their well being. The steward has the responsibility to care for the owner's possessions in such a way that the owner's assets prosper. This is the point of the parable of the three slaves who were given talents to manage while the master was gone (Matthew 25:14-25). The expectation was that the slaves would so manage the money that it would grow. Burying it in the ground was not an acceptable option. But there is more. The steward is also to manage the owner's possessions in such a way that others who depend on the owner receive benefit. In Genesis 43 and 44 these people are Joseph's brothers.

What Does All This Mean for Us Today?

The above material has much to say to our day. I would like to suggest four things, with the first two falling into the category of cautions, and the final two falling into the category of things to be celebrated.

The first caution comes from the strong biblical statement that God is the creator and owner of all that is. Contrasting with this is our cultural language that suggests that each of us is the owner of that which is under our control. People commonly talk about what they "give back to God." This seems to imply that the 5 percent or 10 percent that someone places in the offering plate is God's, and the remaining 95 percent or 90 percent belongs to the individual, and is theirs to do with as they please.

However, if that same person correctly understands that everything, all 100 percent, belongs to God, then that person's faith influences how they make use of all that God has entrusted to them. That is a huge difference. No longer is the question, "How does God want me to use God's 5 percent?" Now the question is, "How does God want me to use everything?" Harry

Wendt pointed to another huge difference in a lecture I heard several years ago. He said, "No longer is the question, 'How much of my money should I give to God?' Now the question is, 'How much of God's money do I dare keep for myself?'"

This first caution has to do with our false sense of ownership. Getting this one wrong can make a true sense of stewardship impossible, because the steward falsely imagines that the owner's property belongs not to the owner but the steward.

The second caution has to do with the false notion that we have what we have because we deserve it, and because we have earned it by our own intelligence and hard work. Remember the words from Deuteronomy 8, "But remember the Lord your God, for it is he who gives you power to get wealth."

Our American culture has trumpeted the "self-made man" at least since the time of Horatio Alger. The rags to riches story of a person who has pulled himself or herself up by the bootstraps and made something out of nothing has a long-standing place in our nation's mythology. We tend to take a very individualistic view of "success," ignoring the multitude of complicated factors that have caused one person to achieve wealth and power, while others have not.

This individualism flies right in the face of Moses' words to the Israelites. It is simply not the case that each of us deserves sole credit for what we have accomplished. Countless forces over which we have no control have helped make us what we are. The brains and the hard work for which we want to take credit are God's, and God entrusts them to us.

Rather than taking credit for my wealth, my wealth ought to cause me to ponder why God has chosen to so bless me. Rather than focusing my life on amassing wealth that dramatically exceeds my needs, I ought to focus my life on using the wealth that God has entrusted to me to help those who have less.

These two cautions are not unique to the American scene. However, given the boundless wealth that exists in our land, they are two cautions that need to guide our stewardship ministry.

They are certainly two cautions that can give a preacher plenty of fodder for a few stewardship sermons.

Those are the cautions. Now what is it that the above pages suggest should be celebrated?

First, we should celebrate the fact that God has named us stewards. To be a steward is to be in a place of high esteem and responsibility. To be God's steward is a privilege like few others. Too often I hear people talk about serving in stewardship ministry in their congregation as if they have drawn the short straw. I sense that if it were a choice between a root canal treatment and serving on the stewardship committee, they might just head for the dentist. This ministry of stewardship is great stuff. Let's celebrate the fact that God has named us stewards. It is an honor and a privilege. Let's celebrate the opportunity to lead a congregation of God's people in being stewards. That too is an honor and a privilege.

Second, we should celebrate the fact that our creator God promises to be with us when we go out in God's name. Therefore, we can know that God has already provided us with all the resources we need to accomplish the mission to which God has called us. Occasionally, I work with a congregation that acts as if God is a God of scarcity, rather than a God of abundance. These congregations lack a vision of what they are called to do in God's name, because they don't think they have the resources to accomplish anything. These congregations sometimes congratulate themselves if the budget for the coming year is smaller than the budget for the current year. This sort of behavior is a slap in God's face. God calls us to great and wonderful things. God provides us generously with the resources we need to do what God calls us to do. Let's celebrate this.

Summary
The goal of our stewardship ministry is to help God's people grow in their relationship with Jesus through the use of the time, talents, and finances God has entrusted to them.

The Old Testament provides the basis for God's people to use their stewardship as a way for their relationship with God to grow. If God's people understand that they are the owners of what they have, or if they understand that they have accumulated resources through their own accomplishments rather than from the good and generous hand of God, then a right understanding of stewardship is almost impossible.

As stewardship leaders, you need to find and utilize ways to help God's people see God as the source—and God's children as the stewards—of all that is under their care. Sermons, talks in worship, and newsletter articles all seem excellent ways to communicate this message. Obviously, this will need to be an ongoing strategy, for a one-time blitz will not impact something so deeply imbedded in our culture.

Chapter 3

Money and Possessions
in the New Testament

JESUS TALKS A LOT ABOUT MONEY AND POSSESSIONS. SEVERAL people have observed that Jesus talks more about money and possessions than about any other topic, except the kingdom of God itself. Jesus talks about money and possessions more than he talks about prayer, more than he talks about his death, more than he talks about forgiveness.

The letters of the New Testament also contain an amazing amount of material about money and possessions. From "God loves a cheerful giver" in 2 Corinthians 9 to "the love of money is a root of all kinds of evil" in 1 Timothy 6, there are many more references to money and possessions in the letters than most would expect.

The reason for this is obvious: Jesus and his early followers are acutely aware that there is an intimate connection between faith and finances, a connection that can either threaten faith or strengthen faith. I have suggested that your stewardship ministry ought to focus on helping followers of Jesus grow in their relationship with Jesus. If you are going to do this, it is important to take seriously what the New Testament has to say about money and possessions.

The teachings of the New Testament regarding money and possessions fall into two general categories. The first is that money and possessions pose a threat to a person's relationship with Jesus. It is clear that the New Testament is convinced that the more money and possessions a person has, the greater the threat. The second is that having money and possessions places on a person the duty to use these to alleviate the needs of those who have little money and few possessions. This chapter will consider these two categories.

The Threat of Money and Possessions

Before looking at specific passages, it is important to talk about why the New Testament is so concerned about money and possessions. The answer can be stated in four words: Jesus wants your heart. Jesus wants nothing more than to be in relationship with you and to have your heart turned toward him. Jesus and others in the New Testament see money and possessions as threats because they can turn one's heart away from Jesus.

Jesus makes this very clear in Matthew 6:24:

> No one can serve two masters; for a slave will either hate the one and love the other, or be devoted to the one and despise the other. You cannot serve God and wealth.

The little sentence, "You cannot serve God and wealth" sums up the threat of having money and possessions. When one has wealth, one is tempted to trust in that wealth. When wealth becomes the object of one's trust, then wealth has taken the place of Jesus Christ, who is the only worthy object of a believer's trust.

In order to grasp the impact of this little six-word sentence, we need first dispel the false myth that we are not rich. Let me state it clearly: If you are reading this book, you are rich. There are many people in our society who are rich beyond most people's ability to comprehend. It is tempting to compare yourself with one of the incredibly rich, and then conclude that you are not really wealthy. When you do this, much that the Bible has to say about the danger of money and possessions loses its punch. You can't get off the hook that easily. You are wealthy.

You are wealthy by any standards. Historically, it has been observed that sometime in the 1950s, western society achieved a standard that had never existed in the history of the world. The majority of people in the western world were not living from hand to mouth. The majority of people had more than enough to meet today's needs, and were thus able to have discretionary income and to save. Fifty years later, this situation has obviously expanded. The majority of people in the western world have considerable discretionary income, and they have way more than enough to cover the costs of food, clothing, and shelter.

We in the western world are also wealthy globally. One of the shocking realizations of people who travel to third-world countries is just how poor most people are. For many, this is a life-changing experience. My own trip to India several years ago changed forever my understanding of my own wealth. I realize that I have more in common with the very wealthy of my own country than I have in common with the average citizen of a third-world country.

I am wealthy, and so are you. When you read passages in the New Testament that talk about the dangers of wealth, you dare not dismiss them, imagining that they are talking about people who are far richer than you are. These passages are talking to you. The dangers described in these passages are dangers you face every day as you strive to live as a disciple of Jesus.

Jesus said, "You cannot serve God and wealth." I am convinced that in the United States we try to do precisely that which Jesus says we cannot do. I firmly believe that we try to do both. We try to serve both God and wealth. Of course we want to serve God, and we also want to place our trust in the security that we think can come from wealth. Dare we call this the American heresy?

Our culture talks to us constantly about financial security. We are advised to buy insurance, to invest in the stock market, to make sure we are saving enough. Our country debates whether or not Social Security should be privatized—and the argument turns on the question, "Will privatization give people more financial security?" Countless articles are written concerning how much money someone needs to have saved in order to retire comfortably. We spend a lot of energy worrying about our financial security.

As we plan for our future, the message that is hammered home to us is, "Make sure you have enough. Make sure you have saved enough, and that you have invested it wisely. That way, you will be able to trust that your future is secure." For most of us, this is just plain common sense. We see absolutely no problem trusting in our financial security for the economic realities of this life, and at the same time trusting in Jesus for our spiritual needs, and for our eternal life.

However, we need to recognize that Jesus says there is a problem here. The problem is the impossibility of serving two masters. Jesus' words are radical: You "will either hate the one and love the other, or be devoted to the one and despise the other" (Matthew 6:24). Our Lord doesn't leave us much middle ground. Our Lord doesn't leave us much "wiggle room." What "just makes sense" to us, causes Jesus to say, "That won't work; you can't do it. If you try to serve money and me, you will either love the money and hate me, or hate the money and love me. Try as you will, you just can't serve both."

The writer of 1 Timothy 6:6-10 offers a powerful commentary on Jesus' words here, saying:

> Of course, there is great gain in godliness combined with contentment; for we brought nothing into the world, so that we

can take nothing out of it; but if we have food and clothing, we will be content with these. But those who want to be rich fall into temptation and are trapped by many senseless and harmful desires that plunge people into ruin and destruction. For the love of money is a root of all kinds of evil, and in their eagerness to be rich some have wandered away from the faith and pierced themselves with many pains.

The last sentence of the paragraph captures Jesus' fear. Jesus doesn't want his children wandering away from him. Jesus doesn't want wealth to become the object of trust that causes one of his beloved to stop trusting in him. This is the bottom line. Jesus wants your trust. He knows that if you try to trust your wealth and him, you are in an impossible situation. Your trust will go one way or the other. You can't do both, and he doesn't want to risk losing you.

An amazing example of the truth of the six-word sentence, "You cannot serve God and wealth" is found in Luke 18:18-25:

A certain ruler asked him, "Good Teacher, what must I do to inherit eternal life?" Jesus said to him, "Why do you call me good? No one is good but God alone. You know the commandments: 'You shall not commit adultery; You shall not murder; You shall not steal; You shall not bear false witness; Honor your father and mother.'" He replied, "I have kept all these since my youth."

When Jesus heard this, he said to him, "There is still one thing lacking. Sell all that you own and distribute the money to the poor, and you will have treasure in heaven; then come, follow me."

But when he heard this, he became sad; for he was very rich. Jesus looked at him and said, "How hard it is for those who have wealth to enter the kingdom of God! Indeed, it is easier for a camel to go through the eye of a needle than for someone who is rich to enter the kingdom of God."

This is a touching and tragic story. It is touching, because Jesus obviously wants this man to be a disciple. In Mark's telling of this encounter, he even reports, "Jesus, looking at him, loved him" (Mark 10:21). Jesus takes a liking to this questioner, and wants desperately for him to do what he needs to do so that he might follow Jesus.

The tragedy, of course, is that what the ruler must do to follow Jesus is precisely the thing that the ruler cannot do—part with his money. Luke tells us he cannot do this because he is very rich. This ruler found the truth of Jesus' words, "You cannot serve God and wealth." In finding that truth, he went away. Sad perhaps, but he still went away from Jesus rather than following Jesus.

One of the characteristics of discipleship in the New Testament is that it involves both a leaving and a following. Disciples must leave behind something, and then they are free to follow Jesus. Perhaps the best example is the call of Peter, Andrew, James, and John in Matthew 4:18-22. Jesus sees them working at their trade, and he calls them from fishing to following. Matthew says of Peter and Andrew, "Immediately they left their nets and followed him" (Matthew 4:20). Of James and John he says, "Immediately they left the boat and their father, and followed him" (Matthew 4:22).

The ruler finds himself in the same situation. He must leave something behind in order to follow Jesus. Unfortunately, he is unable to do that.

It is important to note that Luke implies that were the ruler less wealthy, he might have been able to leave his wealth behind. He seems to be saying not only that one cannot serve God and wealth, but also that the more wealth one has, the more likely it is that wealth will win in the struggle between the two. It is harder to leave lots of possessions than it is to leave a few possessions.

Jesus himself picks up this theme in the last sentences of the section. Jesus said, "How hard it is for those who have wealth to enter the kingdom of God! Indeed, it is easier for a camel to go through the eye of a needle than for someone who is rich to enter the kingdom of God" (Luke 18:25). Since we live in a land of such great wealth, we often are uncomfortable with these words of our Lord, and try to explain them away. We are not alone in this regard. When I was in Israel and Palestine several years ago our guide showed us a rock formation which he said the locals called, "The eye of the needle." It was not large, but perhaps large enough for a small camel to get through. He said it was this formation that Jesus was referring to, and that Jesus meant it was difficult, but not impossible, for a wealthy person to enter the kingdom of God.

These passages from the New Testament, and many, many others stress the threat that money and possessions pose to one's relationship with Jesus. The point of these passages is not that money in and of itself is evil. Rather, the point is that wealth has a way of luring us to trust in it. Wealth has a way of convincing us to stake our future on our accumulation of it. Wealth has a way of tricking us into thinking that without it we are nothing. When we fall into this trap, we have started trusting in something other than our Lord and Savior Jesus Christ.

As stewardship leaders, we need to be honest with ourselves about the role of wealth in our own lives. We also need to help members of the congregation ask tough questions about the role of wealth in their lives. If it is true that in our country a lot of people are trying to serve God and wealth, then we need to confront that, examine it in our lives, and recognize the power of Jesus' teaching: you cannot serve God and wealth.

The New Testament goes even farther when it talks about the threat of wealth. It also warns that if you have to choose between serving God or wealth, choosing wealth is the wrong choice to make, because wealth can't deliver on the promises it makes.

Jesus told a parable often called the Parable of the Rich Fool:

Then he told them a parable: The land of a rich man pro-
duced abundantly. And he thought to himself, "What should
I do, for I have no place to store my crops?" Then he said, "I
will do this: I will pull down my barns and build larger ones,
and there I will store all my grain and my goods. And I will
say to my soul, Soul, you have ample goods laid up for many
years; relax, eat, drink, be merry."

But God said to him, "You fool! This very night your life
is being demanded of you. And the things you have prepared,
whose will they be?" So it is with those who store up treasures
for themselves but are not rich toward God. (Luke 12:16-21)

Before considering what Jesus has to say about this rich
man, we need to recognize that in our society he would be considered a very prudent man. He has taken his wealth, set it aside
to provide for his future, and then plans to settle back and enjoy
the fruits of his labor. In my community, he would be held up
as a role model of a successful businessman, and many would
be jealous of the amount of time he could spend golfing in the
summer and travelling south for the winter. We would long to
emulate him.

Jesus' point, of course, is that this man has placed his trust
in the wrong place. His life may appear quite elegant in the here
and now, but the transitory nature of life is such that it can all be
gone in a minute. Trusting in wealth has lots of allure, because
this world defers to those who have accumulated much. However, as my father used to say, we are all just one breath away
from leaving this world.

Moving from a negative analysis of the situation to the positive analysis, Jesus wants you to have your treasure stored up
with him. Jesus wants you to be his disciple. Jesus wants you to
know the eternal importance of serving God, and not wealth.

The Duty of Being Wealthy

The New Testament also demands the just sharing of resources. It is the duty of those who are wealthy to give generously of their wealth to those who are in conditions of physical need. This duty flows out of the material that we discussed in the last chapter. Since God owns everything, since we are managers of what God has entrusted to us, and since that management exists for the good of others, then it stands to reason that God has blessed the wealthy with material items, not so that they may hoard things for themselves, but rather use that wealth to benefit those who have material needs.

The duty of the wealthy to take action to alleviate the suffering of the poor is a prominent theme of the Old Testament prophets. This theme continues in the New Testament, although the tone of the material does change.

Jesus' parable of the Rich Man and Lazarus (Luke 16:19-31) certainly contains strong language about what will happen to those who ignore the needs of the poor in this life. Jesus' parable of the Sheep and the Goats (Matthew 25:31-46) also stresses the duty to care for those in need. In this parable such caring seems to be a way of life, since those who cared for the poor weren't even aware that in so doing they had been caring for their Lord. Living a life of generosity was simply how they lived.

In the book of Acts it becomes clear that divesting of wealth so that all might have the necessities became common practice. In Acts 2:44-45 we read, "All who believed were together and had all things in common; they would sell their possessions and goods and distribute the proceeds to all, as any had need." Just two chapters later, in Acts 4:34-35, there is another report of such sharing: "There was not a needy person among them, for as many as owned lands or houses sold them and brought the proceeds of what was sold. They laid it at the apostles' feet, and it was distributed to each as any had need."

In 2 Corinthians 8, Paul appeals to the Corinthian Christians with these words, as he asks for their contribution to a collection for the saints:

> I do not mean that there should be relief for others and pressure on you, but it is a question of a fair balance between your present abundance and their need, so that their abundance may be for your need, in order that there may be a fair balance. As it is written, "The one who had much did not have too much, and the one who had little did not have too little." (2 Corinthians 8:13-15)

Through all of these passages and others like them the theme of Christian duty to give generously toward the needs of others emerges. What also emerges is the idea that this is not to be a burden, but rather a consequence of the fact that some have more than they need, while others have less than they need. Generosity is the natural consequence of abundance. When this generosity does not exist, then it is a perversion of God's intention, and comes under attack, whether from the prophets or Jesus.

I would suggest that it is in generosity that we may find a way to deal successfully with the threat of money and possessions. I have found that the most effective way to break the power of money is to give it away—to give it away generously, to give it away in a manner that the world would describe as reckless. In giving money away generously, we are making a bold statement to ourselves and others that we are not serving money, that we have not believed its lies to us about the security that it offers. In giving money away generously, especially to Jesus' work through the church, we are saying we won't try to serve God and wealth. Rather, we will use the wealth that God has entrusted to us for God's ends.

I don't want to be simplistic here. I don't want to fall into the trap of saying that you can give a generous amount to the church, and then cling like crazy to the rest. I don't want to let us off the hook of the money threat too easily, because clearly one could give a tithe and beyond to the church, and still trust in the wealth that accumulates from the ninety percent. Remember, it all belongs to God. We always have to wrestle with how it is in our lives with money, possessions, and faithfully following Jesus. This will be a constant struggle.

I don't want to be simplistic, but I do want to say that one thing we can do to help win the battle against the threat of wealth is to recognize the duty of wealth, and give generously of that which God has entrusted to us. This is not a cure-all, but it is hard to imagine anyone successfully handling the threat of money and possessions without being a generous giver. To cling to possessions, giving a pittance of a percentage of one's income to Christ's church, seems certainly to indicate one who has not broken the hold of the master called wealth.

Generous giving is one step to siding with the master who lasts forever.

Summary

The goal of our stewardship ministry is to help God's people grow in their relationship with Jesus through the use of the time, talents, and finances God has entrusted to them.

The New Testament gets to the heart of understanding stewardship ministry as helping people grow in their relationship with Jesus. The New Testament understands that wealth poses a huge threat to a person's relationship with Jesus. The threat is that wealth beckons us to trust in it for our security, rather than trusting in Jesus. In our society, we often want to have it both ways, trying to trust in Jesus for things spiritual and wealth for things material. Jesus says we can't have it both ways. He says you can't serve God and wealth.

The New Testament also offers us a way to start the process of overcoming this threat—through generous giving. The New Testament, like the Old Testament, tells us that giving of one's wealth to help another who is in need is the duty of a child of God. This duty can become a way of life. Generous giving can break the power of wealth. By giving money away generously we put money in its proper place, and place our trust with the only one ultimately worthy of that trust, Jesus our Lord. Sondra Ely Wheeler, in her book *Wealth As Peril and Obligation*, says it this way: "When the New Testament counsels people to abandon what they own, give their possessions as alms, . . . it is in order that they may do something else: find eternal life, have treasure in heaven, be the children of God, or enter the kingdom" (Grand Rapids: William B. Eerdmans Publishing Company, 1995, p. 147).

Chapter 4

Portrait of a Biblical Giver

At the end of the previous chapter I claimed that generous giving is a key to responding positively to the threat posed by wealth. Going back to chapter 2, we can also confidently say that generosity is one of the characteristics of good stewardship.

In this chapter, I want to explore not only generosity, but other characteristics of a biblical giver. There are certain characteristics that the Bible lifts up when it talks about giving. Developing these characteristics certainly ought to be the goal of all Christian stewards. Since the mission of stewardship ministry is to help people grow in their relationship with Jesus through their stewardship, then it stands to reason that the goal of a congregation's stewardship ministry is to lift up these characteristics and encourage all members to conform their stewardship to them. A question stewardship leaders ought to ask themselves is, "How can we lead this congregation's stewardship ministry so that each member of the congregation is encouraged to ascribe to and practice these biblical stewardship characteristics?"

Another way to think about these characteristics is to think of them as the values of stewardship. When a company develops a mission statement, it often will also develop a list of values, those characteristics by which the company will strive to live. These following six characteristics could easily be seen as the values of a steward.

Value #1: Intentional

Being intentional in one's giving means to develop a plan for your giving and then follow through with that plan. In 2 Corinthians 9:6-7, Paul writes, "The point is this: the one who sows sparingly will also reap sparingly, and the one who sows bountifully will also reap bountifully. Each of you must give as you have made up your mind, not reluctantly or under compulsion." If you are to give as you have made up your mind, then you have to have made up your mind. To be intentional means to make up your mind, to develop a plan for giving, and then to "walk the walk" as you turn that plan into action.

If you find yourself looking in your wallet or purse as you get out of the car on Sunday morning to discover what may be available for the morning offering, then you probably have some work to do on being intentional in your giving. If your giving to church changes from week to week depending on how your checkbook balance is doing, you likely have some work to do on being intentional in your giving.

Most churches use some method for givers to indicate the amount they will give in the coming year. Some call these pledge cards, others call them commitment cards, estimate of giving cards, or faith commitment cards. Whatever you call them, I firmly believe that they are one of the most valuable assets you have in your stewardship ministry.

One of the greatest benefits of these cards is that they help each steward be intentional in giving. Each fall our congregation asks my wife and me to fill out an estimate of giving card for the coming year. After prayer and conversation, we write on that card our giving plan for the next twelve months. Once the new year begins, we give in conformity to the plan we have developed. To quote Paul, we give "as we have made up our mind" (2 Corinthians 9:7). We might be intentional without the estimate of giving card, but it would be more difficult. The discipline of the card helps us be intentional in our giving. It is a gift to us.

A number of years ago I worshiped with a congregation in India. At the time of the offering, after I had gone forward with my offering, I observed others coming forward with their offerings. In many cases, what they put at the altar was food. Often, it was a bag of rice. By the end of the processional offering there was literally a pile of food in front of the altar.

After worship, I asked one of the church leaders about the offering. In particular, I asked about the bags of rice. He said, "The people who worship here are very, very poor. They have no money. So each day, as they prepare food for their families, they put a small amount of rice aside. Each day they add to this amount, and then on Sunday they bring this to the church for their offering. On Monday, we have a food sale for the public, and the proceeds of that sale fund our ministry."

That is intentionality in giving. Those believers have a plan, and they conform to that plan each day as they set aside a small handful of rice for the Lord's work. To be intentional in giving means to develop a plan and then to live the plan.

Value #2: Regular

A second stewardship value is regular giving. To be regular in your giving means to establish a pattern in your giving, and to follow that pattern. Paul puts it this way in 1 Corinthians 16:2, "On the first day of every week, each of you is to put aside and save whatever extra you earn, so that collections need not be taken when I come." Paul's prescribed regular pattern for giving is each week.

As we think about regular giving, we need to recognize that people received income in biblical times very differently than most of us receive income today. In biblical times, it was most common for workers to receive their income at the end of each day. The parable of the generous landowner in Matthew 20:1-16 is an example of this. At the end of the day, all the workers lined up for their pay. To be regular in giving meant a practice similar to what those Indian Christians did with their rice. To be regular in giving meant to set something aside each day and give it in worship each week.

Our system of compensation is different. Some people are paid once a week, others twice a month, others only once each month. Retired people might receive a Social Security check at the beginning of the month, and a pension check some other time. If they are fortunate, they may have income from other investments.

In our day, to be regular in giving means that whenever you receive income, and however you receive income, you give according to your predetermined plan. Obviously, there is a strong connection between intentional giving and regular giving. To be intentional means that you develop a plan for your giving. To be regular means that you follow that plan, according to your own specific way of receiving income.

Value #3: Generous

As I have already indicated, generous giving is perhaps the most basic stewardship value. It is hard to imagine anyone who is serious about discipleship giving one or two percent of his or her income to God's work through the church. It is equally difficult to imagine a tither who isn't serious about discipleship. Generous giving is the *sine non qua* of discipleship.

In Luke 12:34, Jesus says, "For where your treasure is, there your heart will be also." I want to explore this passage further later in this chapter, but for now it is enough to say that if one's treasure is with Jesus, then one's heart is going to be there also. Unfortunately, we need also say that if one's treasure isn't with Jesus, if it is somewhere else, then that person's heart is likely elsewhere as well. These words may sound very "black and white," even harsh. That may be so, but the truth of these words demands that they be spoken.

Paul writes to the Corinthians, "And God is able to provide you with every blessing in abundance, so that by always having enough of everything, you may share abundantly in every good work" (2 Corinthians 9:8). God's incredible generosity is the basis for any call for generous giving on the part of God's people. We can't outgive God. As Christians, one of our key faith statements must be that we will always have enough, because God provides us with all we need. Because God has blessed us so generously, we can, and must, give generously to others, especially those in need.

An incredible story of generous giving is found at the beginning of 2 Corinthians, chapter 8. Paul is appealing to the Corinthians' generosity, and he holds up for them the example of the Macedonian Christians. He writes, "We want you to know, brothers and sisters, about the grace of God that has been granted to the churches of Macedonia; for during a severe ordeal of affliction, their abundant joy and their extreme poverty have overflowed in a wealth of generosity on their part" (2 Corinthians 8:1-2). We would expect Paul to say something like, "their abundant joy and their extreme poverty resulted in them wanting to give generously, but they couldn't." We would expect that, but Paul says something quite different. His comments could be put into a mathematical formula, abundant joy + extreme poverty = wealth of generosity.

In the Evangelical Lutheran Church in America, the average giver gives slightly less than two percent of his or her income to the work of the church. This has serious ramifications for the work that congregations, synods, and the ELCA churchwide can do in mission and ministry. More importantly, it is frightening to think about what this level of giving says about the state of discipleship for the many members of the ELCA who give at this level and below. If one's faith is supposed to yield some signs of its health, and I believe it is, then I worry about the spiritual health of those who are giving at this level. Stewardship leaders don't lack a challenge, do they?

Value #4: First

First-fruits giving is the next stewardship value. This one is easy to understand. Giving first means giving to God first and living off the rest. The opposite, of course, is to take care of the needs and wants of this life first, and give God the leftovers. Deuteronomy 26:1-2 says this:

> When you have come into the land that the Lord your God is giving you as an inheritance to possess, and you possess it, and settle in it, you shall take some of the first of all the fruit of the ground, which you harvest from the land that the Lord your God is giving you, and you shall put it in a basket and go to the place that the Lord your God will choose as a dwelling for his name.

I live in a small town, surrounded by small farms. In the fall it is not uncommon to see a tractor heading into town pulling a trailer heaped with golden yellow corn. My image of giving first would have the farmer swing by the church first, drop off ten percent, and then take the remaining 90 percent to the grain elevator.

That is my image, obviously taken from another era. I'm pretty sure my pastor would not want a pile of grain on the lawn of the church, so we need to translate this image into the twenty-first century. This isn't difficult. Giving first means that when I receive income, the first check I write is to the church. Before I pay my bills, before I head for the grocery store, I write my check to my church. This way, I am certain to give to God first and live on the rest, rather than meeting my wants and needs first and giving God the leftovers.

In the modern world, giving first is an absolutely essential key to giving generously. We live in a world in which advertising is very adept at turning wants into needs. Daily we are bombarded with thousands of messages telling us that we will be happier if only we purchase this product or that. These messages are very sophisticated, and they work. If you don't give to God first, you will short-change God every time. You will use your money in pursuit of this dream or that dream, and God will get what is left.

If you are going to give generously, you need to give first.

Value #5: Proportional

The Bible always calls us to percentage giving. Nowhere in the Bible will you find something like, "Give fifty dollars." The language is always, "Give in proportion to the blessings you have received." Those who have much wealth are expected to give proportionately. Those who have little wealth are also expected to give proportionately. The tithe, or ten percent, is obviously the best example of the Bible's teaching of proportional giving.

Another touching example of proportional giving is found in Mark 12:41-44:

> He [Jesus] sat down opposite the treasury, and watched the crowd putting money into the treasury. Many rich people put in large sums. A poor widow came and put in two small copper coins, which are worth a penny. Then he called his disciples and said to them, "Truly I tell you, this poor widow has put in more than all those who are contributing to the treasury. For all of them have contributed out of their abundance; but she out of her poverty has put in everything she had, all she had to live on."

In terms of actual dollars, the widow's penny is nothing compared to the large sums being put in the offering by the rich. However, in terms of percentage giving, the offering of the poor widow dramatically exceeded the larger sums of the rich. It is this percentage giving that is the standard consistently used in Scripture.

Percentage giving is a two-edged sword. For those who don't have large financial resources, percentage giving is a word of great comfort. Such people can know that in God's eyes their "small" gift is not small at all, but incredibly generous. For those who have greater financial resources, percentage giving calls them to account if their gift is larger in dollars but still quite small in percentage.

It is important for stewardship leaders to stress percentage giving. Doing so is a guard against ever saying unintentionally that someone who can only give today's equivalent of a penny is an insignificant giver. Jesus singled such a giver out for praise. We should do the same. I can think of no greater stewardship tragedy than having a poor widow think that her generous gift is of little consequence. For a poor widow, the gift of $5.00 involves a much greater sacrifice than that experienced by a millionaire who gives $50,000.

Value #6: Cheerful

The final stewardship value is cheerful giving. Perhaps the best-known stewardship verse in the Bible comes from 2 Corinthians 9:7: "God loves a cheerful giver." As you read these words, you may be saying, "Oh, sure! You have just laid five other values on me, I'm feeling guilty about my own giving and that of the other members of my congregation, and now you tell me to be a cheerful giver."

The clue to being a cheerful giver is found in the words that surround Paul's statement that God loves a cheerful giver. Those verses are:

The point is this: the one who sows sparingly will also reap sparingly, and the one who sows bountifully will also reap bountifully. Each of you must give as you have made up your mind, not reluctantly or under compulsion, for God loves a cheerful giver. And God is able to provide you with every blessing in abundance, so that by always having enough of everything, you may share abundantly in every good work. (2 Corinthians 9:6-8)

In the words that surround Paul's appeal for cheerful giving, Paul talks about generous giving, intentional giving, and regular giving. The key to being a cheerful giver is to practice the other stewardship values. If the first five stewardship values characterize your giving, you will be cheerful in your giving. If they don't, you won't. It is that simple.

There was a time many years ago when the first five stewardship values were not in place in my life. I can assure you that the emotions that accompanied my giving did not include being cheerful. I felt guilty, I struggled to write the check to my church, and sometimes I even resented writing that check, small though it was.

At a point in my life, I decided to become a tither, and I decided to follow the other characteristics of biblical stewardship. When I did that, I suddenly began looking forward to writing my check to the church. I enjoyed placing the envelope in the plate. I was excited about what my offering was helping my congregation accomplish. In other words, I was a cheerful giver. Until I conformed my giving to biblical stewardship characteristics, cheerfulness was impossible. After I did, cheerfulness was natural.

Where Your Treasure Is

The six biblical stewardship values—intentional, regular, generous, first, proportional, cheerful—answer the question, "What does a biblical giver look like?" or perhaps more accurately, "How does a biblical giver act?" Encouraging these values in givers is one of the tasks of stewardship leaders in any congregation.

To stress the importance of these biblical values, I want to return to Luke 12:32-34, which we looked at briefly earlier in this chapter:

> Do not be afraid, little flock, for it is your Father's good pleasure to give you the kingdom. Sell your possessions, and give alms. Make purses for yourselves that do not wear out, an unfailing treasure in heaven, where no thief comes near and no moth destroys. For where your treasure is, there your heart will be also.

Many people have misread these words of Jesus and imagined that they say, "For where your heart is, there your treasure will be also." I have even heard people say, "We have to change people's hearts, and then their money will follow." I suppose that could happen, but we need to recognize that this is not what Jesus says.

Jesus says that where your treasure is, where you put your money, that is where your heart will be. If this is true (and who I am to disagree with Jesus?), then we can say that as people grow in their giving to Christ's church, they will grow in their relationship with Jesus. We are talking about a cause-and-effect relationship here. Giving more to Jesus' work will result in growing closer to Jesus. Are we overstating the case if we follow the logic of these verses by saying:

○ Sell your possessions,

○ Give alms,

○ Have treasure in heaven,

○ Have your heart grow closer to Jesus.

Another way to think about what Jesus says here is to talk about "acting your way into a new way of thinking," as opposed to "thinking your way into a new way of acting." If Jesus said, "where your heart is, there your treasure will be also," then he was talking about the need to first change people's hearts. He was talking about trying to think your way into a new way of acting. On the other hand, since what Jesus says here is "where your treasure is, there your heart will be also," then he is talking about the need to first change people's actions. He is talking about trying to act your way into a new way of thinking.

I am convinced it is far easier, and far more lasting to act your way into a new way of thinking. It is far more effective if my actions lead my thoughts, than if my thoughts lead my actions. If I wait until I feel like tithing, I may never get to the action. If, on the other hand, I trust in God's promise, and simply start tithing, I will find that my attitudes toward giving will quickly change. My actions lead my thinking far more effectively than my thinking leads my actions.

What this all means is that what God's people do with their money has a profound impact on God's people's relationship with their Lord. To put it as directly as possible—you have God's promise that if you grow in your giving, you will grow in your relationship with Jesus.

Summary

The goal of our stewardship ministry is to help God's people grow in their relationship with Jesus through the use of the time, talents, and finances God has entrusted to them.

The six stewardship values and Luke 12:32-34 have shown a direct correlation between biblical stewardship practices, especially generosity, and a growing relationship with Jesus. The goal of your stewardship ministry should be for people to live these stewardship values, to increase their giving, not so that your church might have more money, but so that God's children might grow in their relationship with their Lord and Savior Jesus Christ.

Giving intentionally, regularly, generously, first, proportionally, and cheerfully will lead a giver's heart to Jesus. Stewardship leaders have the privilege of asking, "How can we help people become this kind of giver, so that their heart might be drawn closer to Jesus?"

Chapter 5

Practicing Biblical Stewardship

This chapter is a chapter of transition. In these pages we move from the biblical teaching that guides stewardship ministry to the practice of stewardship ministry in your congregation.

It is important to be careful with language here. This is not a transition from the theoretical to the practical. Theoretical sounds like something human beings have concocted that may or may not be true. Obviously, this is a horrible description of God's word. God's word is not theory. Furthermore, what could be more practical than God's word? This is not a transition from the theoretical to the practical. Those are the wrong words.

Biblical teaching guides stewardship ministry. Another word that could be used is *prescribes*—biblical teaching prescribes stewardship ministry. Biblical teaching undergirds everything that you do in stewardship ministry in your congregation. As soon as you separate yourselves from biblical teaching, all is lost. You have separated yourselves from the very core of what you are about.

With this biblical teaching guiding you, now you move into the practice of stewardship ministry. This means that you take the biblical teaching and put it into practice in your congregation—taking into account the history and the context of your congregation. Karl Barth is reported to have said that a preacher climbs into the pulpit with the Bible in one hand and the newspaper in the other. Something like this is what I am suggesting for your stewardship leaders. The biblical teaching guides all that you do, and you provide what only you can provide, a sense of what has happened and what can happen in your congregation.

As we make this transition, I want to consider two topics: the need to talk plainly about money and the role of the pastor in stewardship ministry.

Talk Plainly about Money

If stewardship ministry is going to help people in your congregation grow in their relationship with Jesus through the faithful use of the time, talents, and money that God has entrusted to them, then your congregation is going to have to be a place where there is open, plain talk about money. It ought to be enough to say that we should talk about money because Jesus did. If we are going to say that, then we should be able to take things a little farther and say that we should talk a lot about money because Jesus talked a lot about money.

Unfortunately, there are many cultural taboos that work against open, plain talk about money in congregations. The first is the general societal taboo that tells us that money is a private topic, and that it is no one else's business. Somewhere along the way, around kindergarten, most of us learned that there are three topics that you don't dive into in polite conversation—sex, money, and politics. My own experience is that most people today have little problem expounding their political opinions. Sex is still a taboo, but money is even more so. Most people would rather talk about their sex lives than reveal their net worth or their annual income.

Reluctance to talk about money can place a huge roadblock in the way of stewardship ministry in your congregation. People may be put off by someone who stands before them and says, "I am a tither, and I encourage you to consider tithing." Some people will feel that this person has stepped over the line. Others may say that the speaker is bragging. You may find people reluctant to visit members in their homes to talk about stewardship. Again, the societal taboo says that money is an intensely personal matter, and potential visitors fear that they will step over the line of this taboo. At the bottom of these feelings is the fear of offending someone. The ways that this taboo can block your stewardship ministry are countless.

I would also like to suggest to you a second "money taboo" that is unique to congregations. This taboo says that the financial life of the congregation is separate from the spiritual life of the congregation. This taboo claims that the congregation's financial life is not only separate from the spiritual life, it is inferior to the spiritual life.

According to this taboo, the financial life of the congregation is seen as a necessary evil that is best handled by a small group of people, usually business people who deal with money in their professional lives. The financial life of the congregation should only see the light of day on rare occasions. Everyone knows it is there, and sometimes it has to come out into the open, especially when times are tough and one of the business leaders stands up in worship to tell people to dig deeper because the need is great. Ideally, however, the financial life of the congregation seldom rears its ugly head. This way, God's people can focus their undivided attention on spiritual matters, which is as it should be. So goes the taboo.

This second, uniquely congregational taboo is seldom verbalized, but it is alive and well. My favorite manifestation of it is to look at the glaze that comes over people's eyes when it is announced that it is time for the annual stewardship program. Why is it that the entire congregation can get excited about the beginning of Sunday school, the celebration of Christmas, or a new Lenten series, but when the new stewardship program is announced there is a huge, inaudible groan uttered by all?

Put these two taboos together, and there is strong sentiment in your congregation to not talk about money. Don't give in to that sentiment. As stewardship leaders, you need to make sure that money is talked about plainly and openly.

Jesus and the authors of the New Testament obviously understood that money is a huge issue in people's relationship with their Lord. As we have seen, it can pose real "problems" in that relationship, or it can be a "catalyst in strengthening that relationship." Because of this, we have to talk about money. I guarantee you that if you don't talk about money in your congregation you are assuring that money will be a problem in people's relationship with Jesus. The only way to move money from the problem category into the catalyst to strengthening the relationship category is to talk about money, talk about it openly, and talk about it a lot.

God's people need to talk about money, because talking about money can turn money into a faith-strengthening issue rather than a faith-threatening issue. Don't talk about money only when the congregation needs some. Remember, our focus is not on the congregation's needs, but rather on strengthening the relationship between people and their Lord.

The pages that follow will give you suggestions about how to put this conviction into practice. For now, it is enough to acknowledge this potential roadblock, and to say we have to conquer it. I encourage you to talk with other stewardship leaders in your congregation about these two money taboos. How strong are they in your congregation? How do you see them manifesting themselves?

The Role of the Pastor in Stewardship Ministry

One of the most obvious ways these two taboos play out in congregational life is that many congregations don't want their pastor to be involved in either stewardship ministry or the financial life of the congregation. Furthermore, many pastors would prefer not to be involved in these matters. Let's examine both of these situations.

Many congregations don't want their pastor involved in either stewardship ministry or the financial life of the congregation. If one accepts the spiritual/financial distinction that lies at the heart of taboo number two, then an obvious application of that distinction is that the pastor more than anyone else should limit himself or herself to spiritual matters. More than once I have talked to pastors who have been taken aside by one of the business leaders at the beginning of their ministry in a congregation and told, "Pastor, you don't have to worry about money issues here at First Church. We will take care of the business end of the congregation; you worry about spiritual matters."

Congregations often don't want their pastor involved in the financial matters of the congregation because of the spiritual/financial division that they wrongly imagine exists. I also wonder if there aren't other, more sinister reasons at work. I wonder if congregations don't want the pastor involved in the financial business of the congregation because they are afraid the pastor might want to change things. I wonder if people don't want the pastor involved because the pastor just might find out that people's financial stewardship isn't what it should be.

I also wonder if something far deeper isn't going on here. People don't want the pastor involved because as long as the spiritual/financial division is intact, then people don't have to hold their financial lives up to the light of Scripture. As long as the spiritual/financial division is intact, religion can be kept in a safe box that does not have to impact the business that fills the rest of the week. I also wonder if this isn't about power and control. For those who direct the financial life of the congregation, keeping the pastor out of this realm of the congregation's life preserves the power and control of those who are involved.

Let us not imagine, however, that this is a one-way street. In most cases the pastor is not seeking a central place in the stewardship and financial life of the congregation. There are a number of reasons many pastors would just as soon let the spiritual/financial division remain intact.

First, pastors have been raised with the same taboos as everyone else. Many pastors are no more comfortable talking about money than the people in the pew are. Pastors also know that people can react strongly when they feel a taboo has been violated. Not wanting to go out of their way to make people angry, many pastors would just as soon not talk about money.

Second, pastors know that salaries make up the largest single category in most congregational budgets. They are uniquely aware that talking to people about giving can be perceived as being very self-serving. No pastor would ever want a person to think that the pastor is talking about money just so the pastor can get a raise. Sometimes pastors avoid this possibility by simply not talking about money at all.

Third, some pastors know that their own stewardship house is in disarray, and therefore they aren't comfortable talking to others about stewardship. In some cases, this is a very painful situation for the pastor. A young pastor in her first year of ministry once said to me, "I have fifty thousand dollars in school loans. By the time I make my school loan payment, my car payment, buy groceries and the few other things I need, I'm out of money. I can't even think about tithing, so how in the world can I ask the members of the congregation to do something I'm not doing?" In other cases, pastor's stewardship houses are in disarray because they have never learned what it means to be a good steward. In either case, pastors who can't be—or simply aren't—good givers are very unlikely to talk about financial stewardship.

Some congregations don't want their pastor to talk about money. Some pastors don't want to talk about money. In the book, *Plain Talk about Churches and Money* (The Alban Institute, 1997, p. 130), Loren Mead talks about a "conspiracy of silence" in this matter. The "conspiracy of silence" is an often unspoken agreement that everyone will be more comfortable if money isn't talked about in the congregation, especially by the pastor. As long as this conspiracy of silence holds, then we can continue to imagine that the financial/spiritual distinction holds. As long as this distinction holds, our relationship with Jesus and our openness to joyful, abundant giving will be limited.

When the financial part of our lives is shielded from our relationship with Jesus, then finances will always be a problem for that relationship. As long as we imagine that finances and faith don't mix, then some of God's people will wrongly imagine that what they do with their money has nothing to do with their relationship with Jesus. Some will want to keep it this way, and therefore will get angry if their pastor insists on talking about money and getting involved in the stewardship ministry of the congregation. On the contrary, it is precisely for this reason that the pastor must talk about money and be involved in the stewardship ministry of the congregation.

The pastor needs to shatter the "conspiracy of silence" by talking about money. The pastor must do this for the spiritual health of the people in the congregation. As long as the pastor refuses to shatter the "conspiracy of silence," then the conspiracy will continue. Because of the unique position of the pastor, he or she alone is in the position to end the false spiritual/financial dichotomy.

How should the pastor talk about money? How should the pastor be involved in the stewardship ministry of the congregation? In some congregations, very carefully and very gradually. In other congregations, the situation may allow the pastor to move naturally into these two areas. Pastors and lay leaders should have an open and candid conversation about this matter, and together determine a plan of action. Some helpful suggestions are:

The pastor should preach on stewardship issues when the assigned text deals with these issues. Since the Gospels talk so much about money and possessions, it is inevitable that the assigned gospel will occasionally contain one of these passages. When this happens, the pastor should preach on the text forthrightly. It is important to note that these texts will not lead the pastor to talk about the need of the church to receive. Rather, these texts will talk about the need of each worshiper to consider their finances in the light of their relationship with Jesus, and the need of each worshiper to give generously of that which God has entrusted to them. This is an important distinction, and can blunt some of the criticism that the pastor is always asking for money.

The pastor must be a part of the stewardship leadership team. When a pastor talks to me about the stewardship team by saying, "they do this," I know that stewardship ministry in that congregation is not what it could be. Stewardship ministry is too important to the spiritual lives of the members of the congregation for the pastor to not be involved. Because of his or her biblical and theological training, the pastor is uniquely positioned to keep the stewardship team on track, understanding stewardship ministry to be about the need of the giver to give and not the need of the church to receive. The pastor simply must be a key stewardship leader.

The pastor should model effective stewardship. Despite all the cultural taboos, the pastor needs to talk about money, and talk about his or her own personal financial stewardship. If the pastor is tithing or beyond, the congregation should know that. If the pastor has circumstances in his or her life that block this, the congregation should know about them. One of my great stewardship mentors was a colleague in my first call. Pastor Dan Sander talked so honestly and openly about money and about his personal stewardship that I don't think it ever occurred to anyone that he shouldn't be doing this. His caring candor defused the taboos.

The pastor should know what each person gives to the congregation. I am aware that in some congregations this is the final taboo. I have heard the common complaint, "If the pastor knows how much people give, the pastor will let this influence his or her ministry to people. He or she will cater to the big givers." My standard answer to this is that if your pastor would structure pastoral care around giving levels, then you have much bigger problems than what the pastor does or doesn't know.

Because wealth and what we do with the money and possessions God has entrusted to us is such a huge issue in our relationship with Jesus, the pastor has to know what people give. How is the pastor to help people grow in their relationship with Jesus if he or she is kept in the dark about how much people give? The pastor needs to have access to giving information, and the pastor needs to handle this information just as the pastor handles everything else the pastor knows about people's lives—confidentially and pastorally.

Three Key Verbs

The rest of this book is going to suggest a way for you to structure your congregation's stewardship ministry. The structure is going to focus on three verbs. These verbs are ask, thank, and tell. I will encourage you to have three subgroups on your stewardship leadership team. Each subgroup will be responsible for carrying out the activities implied by one of the three verbs.

"Ask" describes all the different ways people in your congregation are asked to consider the blessings God has entrusted to them, and how they feel called to respond to those blessings through generous giving. "Thank" describes all the ways your congregation acknowledges with appreciation the generous response of those who support the ministry you do together. "Tell" describes the many ways the congregation is made aware of the wonderful work you do together, and how important each person's support is to the ongoing work of ministry.

Summary

The goal of our stewardship ministry is to help God's people grow in their relationship with Jesus through the use of the time, talents, and finances God has entrusted to them.

If congregational life is going to contribute to this growth in people's relationship with Jesus, then money needs to be a topic of open, plain talk. As long as money is not a topic of conversation, money will continue to be a problem in people's relationship with Jesus, rather than a catalyst for strengthening that relationship. Because of cultural and congregational taboos, there will always be people who want money on the list of topics that aren't talked about in the congregation.

Stewardship leaders need to lead in this regard, insisting that money is not only an appropriate, but a necessary, topic for conversation. Key in this is the role of the pastor. The pastor needs to have a central place in the stewardship ministry and the financial life of the congregation. If a congregation resists this, the pastor can't overcome this resistance by himself or herself. Stewardship leaders will need to be dependable allies in making this change.

Chapter 6

Ask: The Annual Response Program

THE NEXT THREE CHAPTERS WILL FOCUS ON HOW THE members of your congregation are asked to respond to the blessings God has entrusted to them. The annual response program (also known as the "stewardship program" in many congregations) is the cornerstone of your stewardship ministry. The annual response program is that time each year when members of the congregation are asked to consider the blessings God has entrusted to them and how they will respond to those blessings through financial support of the congregation's ministry.

I am aware that some recent literature suggests that the day of the annual response program may have passed. In some congregations this may be true. However, I am convinced that in the vast majority of congregations, the annual response program continues to be a vital time of stewardship education and financial response to God's blessings.

It is important to think of the annual response program as the cornerstone of your stewardship ministry. As the cornerstone, it is vital. It is hard to imagine a congregation having effective stewardship ministry without some sort of annual response program. Members of your congregation need the reflection and the challenge that an annual response program provides.

As the cornerstone, the annual response program is not the whole building. Unfortunately, there are too many congregations where the Stewardship Committee meets for the first time in August and members look at each other across a table and ask the question, "It's that time again. What are we going to do this fall?" This approach won't get the job done. The annual response program needs to have its prominent place among a host of building blocks that together will construct an effective stewardship ministry in your congregation.

Don't Forget the Basics

As you start to think about your annual response program, don't forget the basics. As the tire commercial of a generation ago said, "this is where the rubber meets the road." As you start the practice of stewardship ministry, make sure to remember that you are putting into practice the biblical teaching that has been considered in the previous chapters. If the material in those chapters has been new to your congregation's stewardship ministry, you will have the hard work of doing things in a new way. That is hard work, and it may take some time, but it is absolutely essential work. Don't slip back into old habits if old habits were driven by focusing on the church's need to receive member's money.

Remember your mission statement. Your work is about helping people grow in their relationship with Jesus through their financial stewardship. In the Old Testament, when God wants his people to never forget something, God instructs them to "fix it as an emblem on your forehead" (Deuteronomy 6:8). At the risk of irreverence, I want to encourage you to fix this mission statement as an emblem on your forehead. Don't ever forget it as you move into the practice of your congregation's stewardship ministry. Your goal is to focus on the giver, on the disciple, and on the marvelous potential that financial stewardship has to help that disciple grow in his or her relationship with Jesus.

What are some of the basics that can help you do this in your annual response program?

Be biblical. God's word is one of the most powerful ways that God speaks to God's people. God's word challenges, encourages, causes growth. As we have seen, both the Old and New Testaments are full of stewardship material. Make sure that God's word has a prominent place in your annual response program. You will probably want to have a theme verse. Newsletter articles and talks in worship should have God's word at their heart. Make sure people have the opportunity to hear what God's word has to say about how they are to live with possessions, with money, with wealth.

Never use a budget. I've talked about this already, so this is just a reminder. At no point in your annual response program should you put next year's budget in front of people. A page full of numbers causes most people's eyes to glaze over in a blank stare. A budget will motivate only a very small percentage of your congregation. Putting a budget in front of people will limit their giving. If you have a five percent increase in your budget for next year, putting a budget in front of the congregation will effectively limit your request to a five percent increase. Remember, the focus is not on the church's need to receive, but on the giver's need to give. Therefore, don't use a budget, use Scripture.

Ask for growth. As I work with congregations in stewardship ministry, I am amazed how often stewardship leaders forget to ask people to grow in their giving. If you don't ask people to grow in their giving, they probably won't. If you do ask people to grow in their giving, my experience is that many, often close to 50 percent a year, will indeed increase their financial response.

There are many tools to help you ask people to grow in their giving. Percentage giving charts provide an easy way for people to figure out their current percentage of giving and encourages givers to grow by one percent per year. Giving step charts breaks down levels of giving into many small steps and asks givers to move up to the next step in giving. Whether you use one of these tools or not, make sure your annual response program includes an invitation to people to grow in their giving.

A word of caution here—I have been regularly amazed at how people will not do even the most simple mathematical calculations in order to discover either their present level of giving or a percentage increase for the coming year. As you ask for growth, you will need to find ways to do the math for people. Asking people to do a simple three-step calculation is probably asking for something that will not happen.

Use estimate of giving cards. Inviting givers to complete an estimate of giving card on which they indicate their level of financial support for the congregation's ministry for the coming year is a central and vital part of the annual response program. The act of filling out the card provides givers an opportunity to consider how God is blessing them and how they want to respond to those blessings. Filling out the card involves planning. Filling out the card provides a level of commitment to which the giver can then hold himself or herself accountable in the coming year.

Although our focus is on the giver, the use of estimate of giving cards also provides many benefits to your congregation. People who use estimate of giving cards each year are more likely to increase their giving. Over time, this will provide considerably more financial resources to fund your congregation's ministry. The use of estimate of giving cards allows your congregation to develop a realistic financial plan for the coming year. When people increase their giving to the congregation, congregational leaders can take that increase into account, and can plan for growth in ministry, knowing that the income will be there to support this growth. When there is no way of knowing about an increase, leaders usually plan conservatively for the future, which only encourages members to give what they gave last year.

Estimate of giving cards are good for the giver, and good for the congregation.

Be clear and direct. Don't beat around the bush. This can be a real temptation. I remember working with a congregation as it conducted its first annual response program. I knew exactly how the program was supposed to work. I was present on the Sunday when people were to fill out their estimate of giving cards. The leader of the program stood up to give his talk in worship. To put it politely, he "chickened out." Standing before the congregation he found himself very uncomfortable talking about money, abandoned his prepared comments, and weakly ad libbed. It was a disaster.

Fortunately, this sort of event is rare, but we do need to be mindful of the importance of being clear and direct. Financial stewardship is about money, so we need to be prepared to talk about money. Annual response programs require people to follow some directions, so we need to be clear when we give those directions. One of the great mistakes church leaders make is to assume that the person in the pew knows as much about what is going on in the congregation as the leaders do. Don't make this mistake. Be clear and direct as you invite people to participate in the annual response program.

Go first class. Every member of your congregation receives high quality print material in their homes each week. They are accustomed to this. Make sure the materials you use in your annual response program are of high quality. This doesn't mean full color and glossy paper. In fact, in most congregations, this would backfire. It does mean that your materials should be laid

out well on the page, free of mistakes, eye catching, and interesting. You have people in your congregation who can do this
sort of work, and do it well. Desktop publishing programs have
allowed many people to do quality work that was previously
unimaginable. Make sure your annual response program uses
materials that are high quality.

Plan-Conduct-Follow Up-Thank

A well-run annual response program requires hard work. Organization and follow-through will enable your program to run
smoothly, and will help members reflect on God's blessings and
make a prayerful response. The following four steps can guide
you in your work.

Step #1: Plan your annual response program. If you conduct
your annual response program in the fall, don't wait until September when everyone is back from vacation to ask, "What
should we do this year?" Plan before everyone goes on vacation.
Four to five months before the beginning of your program is
when you should start planning. Gather your stewardship leaders together and ask some basic questions.

- *What?* What response program will we use this year? Consider what programs you have used in the past five years.
  Don't use the same program more than three consecutive
  years. Will you use the same response method as last year,
  or a new one? Spend some time together in prayer, asking
  for God's guidance as you consider this question. After you
  make a decision, order the materials you will need.

- *When?* Pick the time when you will ask people to complete
  their estimate of giving cards. Depending on the program, this
  may be a Sunday morning, an evening or series of evenings,
  or perhaps even spread over a two-week period. Check the
  church calendar. Look at the three weeks ahead of the time

when people will complete their cards. Will you be able to have talks in worship those Sundays? Make sure you get your dates on the calendar so other committees know your plans.

○ *Who?* Who will be needed to lead the response program? Will your committee members be the leaders, or will you need others to be involved in leadership positions? If you need others, now is the time to recruit them.

Six weeks before the beginning of your program you should gather your leaders again. Now the planning needs to be very specific. If you use a prepared annual response program, it will probably provide detailed guidance as to what planning you need to undertake. At the very least, you should do the following:

○ *Develop a time line.* You should discuss your program in detail and make a time line. What are all the tasks that need to be accomplished? When should they be accomplished? Who will be doing them? Make sure to include things like talks in worship, newsletter articles, bulletin inserts.

○ *Recruit more people.* If people other than the committee members will be giving talks in worship—recruit them now. By the way, it is good to spread this responsibility around. Seeing new faces helps worshipers pay closer attention. If you will be asking the church secretary to help out with some work, make sure someone talks to him or her so there are no last minute surprises.

○ *Order materials.* If you need additional materials, order them now. Don't forget the estimate of giving cards.

Step #2: Conduct your annual response program. Your program should be conducted over approximately three weeks. Longer than this, and the program can lose energy. Shorter than this and you will miss too many people who may be gone from worship for a week or two.

Leading up to asking people to complete their estimate of giving cards, you should have three weeks of inspiration, information, and encouragement. Each week could have a different theme. Each week you could send a letter to congregation members, have a talk in worship, and use a bulletin insert. Remember to stress biblical themes each week. Don't worry about people getting too much information. Repetition and variations on the theme are good.

When the time comes to ask people for their response, make sure everyone knows exactly what is expected of them. Don't assume people know what the directions are. Even if you are doing the same program as last year, you will have some new members. Furthermore, people will forget the details. Be clear in your directions. Just a reminder—in all of this, ask people to consider increasing their giving. God's blessings haven't become static, neither should God's peoples' giving.

Step #3: Follow up with those who haven't returned an estimate of giving card. You should have your follow-up plans in place long before the program begins. If you wait until after most people have completed their estimate of giving cards before you even think about follow-up, it will be too late. You may want to consider having one member of your team whose sole responsibility is to follow-up.

Your follow-up should occur quickly after the majority of cards are returned. Don't wait three weeks, or all connection with the rest of your response program will be lost. Consider writing a letter to those who haven't responded, and including an estimate of giving card and an envelope addressed to the church. Putting a stamp on the envelope is helpful, but certainly not necessary. If you don't get a response to your letter, don't do any more follow-up. If it is perceived that you are badgering, you will have done more harm than good.

Step #4: Thank all who have returned an estimate of giving card. Chapter 9 will go into much greater detail regarding thanking. For now, let me say that it is very important that you quickly thank those who have returned an estimate of giving card. In some congregations, the pastor writes this letter. Often the first paragraph talks about the high points in the congregation's ministry the past year. The second paragraph lays out the pastor's hopes and dreams for the ministry in the coming year. The third paragraph thanks the members for their estimate of giving. The exact amount of the estimate should be included in the letter. This provides the member with the opportunity to make a correction if a mistake has been made in recording their giving plan for the coming year.

Annual Response Program Examples

As your stewardship leadership team considers which annual response program to use, you will have many options. In general, you will be best served by using an already prepared program, and following its directions closely. There are many such programs available that have an excellent track record. These programs have been developed and refined, so don't succumb to the temptation to change them. Use them as written, and they will provide the best results for you.

Annual response programs are distinguished by where the giver is when he or she is asked to complete an estimate of giving card. Most often the three week preparatory period that I have described above is pretty much the same in all of them. I will list and describe each of the seven types. I will not list specific programs in each category, because new programs are becoming available all the time, and some existing programs will not be available in the future.

Commitment at worship

In this type of program, the giver completes his or her estimate of giving card as a part of the Sunday worship. Usually, there is a time allotted in the service for cards to be completed, and then a processional offering occurs, during which the estimate of giving cards are brought forward. In many programs of this type there is a celebration meal following worship during which the preliminary results of the program are announced.

The strengths of this type of program include the connection of the act of filling out the estimate of giving card with the offering as an act of worship. Another strength compared to some other types is that more people are likely to attend worship than will attend an evening meeting or a meeting in someone's home. This is especially true if publicity has been good, if the celebration meal after worship is substantial and if people have made reservations for the meal.

The challenge of this type is that in most congregations only 30 percent of the members are in worship on any given Sunday. This means that even with strong publicity and a great meal, only 40-50 percent will be in attendance. A well-planned follow-up is a must.

Relay

In the relay method, congregation members pass a packet of stewardship materials from home to home. In this packet is an envelope of materials for each household. When the packet arrives, the members find their envelope, read the materials, complete their estimate of giving card, seal it in an envelope and return it to the packet. When they have done this, the packet is passed on to the next home on the list.

The strength of this type of program is that it reaches most givers. Since the materials come to the giver rather than the giver coming to worship or a meeting, the response rate should be high. This program is also very non-threatening. Givers are able to complete their estimate of giving card in the comfort of their own living room.

The challenges of this type of program are several. First, there is no guarantee that the stewardship message will be received. People don't have to read the materials that are intended for them in the packet. Second, since givers don't have to make a commitment of time to participate in the program, they are less likely to increase their financial commitment. Third, some givers will set the packet aside and forget about it. Because of this, it is important to have someone tracking the progress of each packet, so it can be kept moving.

Fellowship meal

In this program congregation members are invited to attend a meal either in the church building or in a community building. At this event, in addition to the meal there is a program on stewardship and the opportunity for the giver to complete an estimate of giving card. The program usually includes both a focus on biblical teaching and a focus on the ministry of the congregation.

The strength of this program is getting the congregation together for a meal event which is an enjoyable group-building experience. The program also offers an excellent opportunity to focus on biblical teaching and to talk about the ministry of the congregation in a way that is uplifting and encouraging.

The challenge of this method, not surprisingly, is attendance. This type of program puts a lot of eggs in the basket of one event, and often only 20 percent of the congregation will attend. Good publicity is key. So is asking people to make a reservation for the meal. If your congregation is large enough, you might want to consider multiple events on different days at different times. Follow-up is very important with this type program.

Dessert and prayer

Dessert and prayer is similar to the fellowship meal type, except instead of a full meal people eat only dessert. Along with dessert, participants join in a program of biblical stewardship and reflection on the congregation's ministry.

The strengths of dessert and prayer are its ease of preparation, and the flexibility afforded by a less formal meal setting. With dessert and prayer it is much easier to schedule multiple events in the hopes that one will fit into everyone's schedule. In large congregations, dessert and prayer provides the opportunity to have a stewardship meeting in a more manageable-sized group.

The challenge of dessert and prayer is again attendance. Good publicity is key. It is more difficult to ask people to make a reservation for dessert, so this is a drawback compared to the fellowship meal. However, the ability to schedule more events may offset this drawback. Again, follow-up will be very important.

Home gatherings

With this program type, members who live in proximity to one another are invited to a meeting in one of their homes. At this meeting, a snack or dessert is served and a program is presented, again focusing on biblical stewardship and the congregation's ministry. Estimate of giving cards are completed at the meeting, placed in an envelope and returned to the program leader.

Strengths of this type of program include the value of an informal gathering in someone's home. Neighborhood community used to be a given. It no longer is. This program can help neighbors connect through their congregation. Another strength is that the number of program leaders increases. This may be seen as a recruitment challenge, but once these leaders are recruited, their training and the act of leading a meeting can become important in helping build the leader's own relationship with Jesus through stewardship.

The main challenge—you guessed it—is attendance. This can be helped if each host sends a personal invitation to those invited to their home and calls all who are invited to their home to secure a response regarding their attendance at the meeting.

A second challenge is developing a program that can be effectively presented by a larger number of leaders. The use of a video presentation can help in this regard, although it is less personal than a program actually presented by the leader.

Home visits

In this program visitors, usually in groups of two, go to the homes of congregation members, present a stewardship message, and ask for estimate of giving cards to be completed, placed in an envelope and returned to them. Years ago, this was the standard stewardship response program. Today, it is much less common, although it continues to be a very effective program.

The strengths of this program are that it involves a large number of people in leading the program, it takes the stewardship message to people so participation is high, and it provides an opportunity for God's people to talk face to face about stewardship and about the congregation's ministry. Because people are visited in their homes, follow-up is greatly reduced.

The challenges of this program are that it requires lots of people and is a lot of work. This is good news. It is also bad news, because if people aren't totally committed to making the program work, it can quickly fall apart. The most common problems are not recruiting enough visitors and not adequately training visitors.

There are two variations of this program that might be considered. The first uses relational visits—that is, visitors visit people with whom they have something in common. They might be neighbors or have children in the same school or be employed in a similar field. The relationship provides a starting point for the conversation and makes the entire conversation easier. Often, when congregations use relational visits, the goal is not to visit the entire membership in a given year, but rather to spread the visits out, visiting each member once in three years.

A second variation has the members come to the church for their face-to-face visit with two "visitors." In our day when many people are uncomfortable having others come into their homes, visiting at the church reduces some of the anxiety. Also, since the visitors aren't driving from visit to visit, visits can be completed in much less time. This means either less time commitment for each visitor, or the possibility for each visitor to complete more visits.

Mail

Some congregations have conducted their stewardship response program entirely by mail. Temple talks and bulletin inserts may still be used for those who attend worship, but the estimate of giving cards are distributed by mail and members are asked to mail the completed card back to the church.

The only strength of this program is that it is relatively easy. The challenges of this method are many. Its relative ease is offset by the fact that it is very impersonal and has a very low response rate. The opportunity to ask people to think about what the Bible has to say about stewardship or to consider the congregation's ministry are severely reduced with a mail program. Follow-up is also difficult. Since the request for a response has occurred by mail, it is unlikely that a follow-up letter is either going to be well received or have much additional success.

I include a mail program here because some congregations try them. My suggestion is that you not join their ranks.

Summary

The goal of our stewardship ministry is to help God's people grow in their relationship with Jesus through the use of the time, talents, and finances God has entrusted to them.

The annual response program is the cornerstone of your congregation's stewardship ministry. This is so because in this program God's children who are members of the congregation have the greatest opportunity to consider the blessings God has entrusted to them, and how they feel called to respond to those blessings by supporting God's work through your congregation. In the annual response program stewardship leaders have the greatest opportunity to be guided by the mission statement.

It is in the annual response program, more than in any other aspect of your stewardship ministry, that the biblical teachings discussed in the first four chapters of this manual come to the fore. It is also here where the greatest threat to abandoning those teachings exists. If your congregation has based past response programs on giving to the need of the church, then you will have hard, but very fruitful work ahead of you.

Be prayerful, be thoughtful, give your best work as you plan, conduct, follow-up, and thank in your annual response program.

Chapter 7

Ask: Making the Pie Larger

As I said in the previous chapter, the annual response program is the cornerstone of your congregation's stewardship ministry. The program is not the end of your congregation's stewardship ministry. In too many congregations, the stewardship leadership team plans and conducts the annual response program, and then takes a break for several months until it is time to start planning next year's program.

The plain truth is that most members of your congregation are not finished giving when they have placed their envelope in the offering plate on Sunday morning. They will receive many additional requests for gifts from many different organizations, and they will respond generously to several of those requests. It only makes sense that some of those additional opportunities to give should come through your congregation.

One way to think of stewardship is to think about making the pie larger. Sometimes my family ends up with a pie on the kitchen counter that has come from the local grocery store. Although these pies don't fall into the "as good as mother used to make" category, some of them are pretty good. What strikes me about them, especially when they are good, is how small they are. Most of them come in 8-inch pie plates. When a homemade pie finds its way to our counter, it is not only "as good as mother used to make," it is also in a 9-inch or even 10-inch pie plate. There's nothing like great pie, and lots of it.

Can we think of the regular Sunday offering as an 8-inch pie? It is wonderful, but there are larger pie plates out there. Giving beyond the regular Sunday offering helps God's people move from 8-inch-pie-plate giving to 10-inch-pie-plate giving.

At the heart of God's people's growing generosity is God's incredible generosity to God's people. God entrusts to us more generously than we can imagine. God stirs our hearts with the story of a wonderful ministry that we want to support. Requests for additional giving recognize these two facts and seek to provide opportunities for trustees of God's generosity to respond to those stories that stir their hearts.

Not everyone will respond to every invitation. That is okay, and it should be expected. Different people will be at different places in their lives every time they are asked to give. Some people, because of their life's history, will be moved by a story of ministry that will not so move other people sitting in the same pew. Invitations for additional giving are exactly that—invitations.

Before turning to various types of additional giving opportunities that you will want to consider, I want to raise a couple of general questions.

How Often Should We Have a Special Offering?

This is a difficult question to answer in a specific way. You will need to consider your congregation's history of special offerings. If you have had no such history, you will want to go slowly at first.

I remember a conversation with a woman who objected to the whole idea of special offerings. As we talked, she described her experience in a former congregation. She told of a weekly request for money coming as a part of the announcements. Each week, it seemed to her, the pastor would stand up, describe a special ministry, and ask the ushers to pass the plates. She was turned off. I suspect I would have been as well. Weekly special offerings are clearly too much.

On the other hand, I know of another congregation that conducts a "harvest offering" that is the only special offering it has each year. A once-a-year harvest offering is not frequent enough for special offerings.

In general, a good guideline is to have a monthly special offering that is well-conducted and provides lots of information about the ministry being supported. Many congregations follow this pattern, and do so quite effectively.

How Can We Combine Giving and Serving?

Special giving opportunities provide members of your congregation with an incredible opportunity to combine giving with serving. As God's people hear stories of ministries that are making a difference in people's lives, they will find themselves wanting to support these ministries financially. As they support these ministries financially and hear even more about the ministry, they may want to support the ministry by giving of their time and talents as well. The connections that begin with a financial gift may well lead to a personal involvement that becomes a powerful act of discipleship and changes the giver's life.

The congregation where I am a member has a strong connection with a ministry in Jamaica. This connection started with an offering. As people heard about the ministry and financially supported it, they wanted to get involved. A group of people went to Jamaica to volunteer for a week. Now this is an annual event for our congregation. What started as a small gift to a special giving opportunity has grown into a powerful act of discipleship for many people. Those who have gone to Jamaica have told their stories, and the connection between our congregation and that ministry has enriched the lives of even those who have not personally made the trip.

My point is obvious: Strive to find ways for members of your congregation to grow their connection to special giving opportunities from merely financial to include time and talents. In the case of a local food shelf or Habitat for Humanity chapter, this should be very easily accomplished. In the case of a ministry halfway around the world, it will take more work. Do what you can. These connections and participation in ministry are almost always powerful discipleship-growing events.

Giving from Regular Income

Opportunities for additional giving typically fall into two categories—giving from regular income and giving from accumulated assets. These two categories are not hard and fast. In almost every case, some will be giving from regular income, while others are giving from accumulated assets. The categories, however, are still helpful.

Additional giving opportunities from regular income generally provide people with the opportunity to support a ministry beyond the ministry of the local congregation. While the Annual Response Program supports the ministry of the congregation, these opportunities support other worthwhile ministries. As you plan stewardship ministry in your congregation, you will want to consider the following opportunities for additional giving from regular income.

Mission of the month

To establish a mission of the month program, your stewardship leadership team will select twelve different ministries that members of the congregation will have the opportunity to support. The twelve ministries should include a blend of local, national, and even global opportunities. One of these ministries is highlighted each month. The story of the ministry can be told through newsletter articles, bulletin inserts, and talks in worship. Throughout the month members are encouraged to place their loose change (paper money is also always welcome!) in a receptacle that is available each Sunday morning. (In one congregation, for example, the receptacle is a "parking meter" that has a slot in the top and a long hollow stand). Often congregations receive an additional offering one Sunday each month for the ministry being highlighted. This can be done by passing the plates at the beginning of worship, or by having a basket out for people as they leave worship.

Mission of the month is a very effective way to raise people's awareness of ministries beyond the local congregation, and to raise financial support for very important work being done by God's people around the world. Mission of the month offers wonderful opportunities to connect giving with serving, as has been discussed above. Mission of the month has worked very well in congregations of less than fifty worshipers as well as those with several hundred worshipers. Many of the ideas found in the balance of this section could be incorporated into a mission of the month program.

Sponsorships

Sponsorships offer people opportunities to support a ministry by signing up to contribute a set amount for a one-week sponsorship. Often, these sponsors are recognized in either the worship bulletin or the newsletter. Many congregations use an annual calendar on which givers can sign up to be a sponsor. Sponsorships are frequently given in memory of someone, in honor of someone, or in honor of an event in someone's life like a birthday, an anniversary, or a graduation. Ministries that might be supported through sponsorships include a missionary, radio, or cable television broadcast of worship, or any other ongoing commitment the congregation chooses to support in this manner.

Regular appeals

Regular appeals are annual appeals that the congregation uses to raise money to support a ministry. These appeals occur at approximately the same time every year. Members of the congregation have a history of supporting these appeals, and expect them to continue in the future. In fact, should one of these appeals disappear, many would miss the opportunity to give to the particular ministry. Examples of these regular appeals would include giving to fight world hunger, giving to the local food shelf, giving to support a Bible camp with which the congregation is connected, or giving to a new ministry the congregation is supporting.

It is important to see these regular appeals as mini-annual response programs.

○ Care should be taken to tell the story of the ministry being supported. Recipients of this sort of offering almost always have extensive material available that interprets the work they do.

○ Make sure you use a variety of ways to ask people to support the ministry. Envelopes could be sent with the newsletter to accompany an article about the ministry. A special mailing could go to all members and non-members who have supported this ministry in the past. Envelopes could be distributed and gathered during worship.

○ Don't forget to thank those who give. Often in these appeals checks are made out to the congregation then consolidated into one check to be sent to the ministry being supported. If this is the case, either the congregation should thank givers or names and addresses of givers should be sent to the ministry so the ministry can thank them.

Special needs

There are times when a need cries out for support. Many national denominations have programs that provide a vehicle for people to help in times of catastrophic need. When a famine fills the news, when a hurricane or flood wreaks havoc on communities, when a national disaster such as September 11, 2001, occurs—such events touch peoples' hearts, and make them want to do something to help. Your congregation should be a place where people can give, confident that their gift is making a difference, and that your denomination will be a good steward of their gift.

Unfortunately, it is likely that more than once a year such a special need will emerge. Your stewardship leaders should be prepared for this. A plan should be in place that authorizes someone to make an immediate decision to conduct such an offering on Sunday morning. The only caution here is to remember the story of the woman who felt that every time she went to worship she was confronted with a special offering. Beyond this, special-needs offerings provide worshipers a way to make a difference in the face of human suffering.

Giving from Accumulated Assets

Gifts from accumulated assets usually come at specific times in the life of the individual or the congregation. They are often specialized gifts and require the assistance of a person trained in such gifts. They are beyond the scope of this book, but since they are such an important part of the stewardship ministry of a congregation, I want to touch briefly on them.

Capital fund appeals

Capital fund appeals are the most frequent opportunities members have to give from accumulated assets. Long-standing, stable congregations may go decades between capital fund appeals, while newer, growing congregations may have more than one capital fund appeal each decade. There are several things to consider regarding capital fund appeals.

- ·◯ Don't try to do them in-house. There are numerous consulting firms that provide expert assistance to congregations during capital fund appeals. Many denominations also offer expert assistance for such appeals. The use of outside assistance will insure a well-run program. Furthermore, most congregations find that the cost of outside assistance is more than covered by the increased financial support generated from those who pledge to the project.

- ◯ Don't view capital fund appeals only as a way to raise money for a building project. A capital fund appeal should be seen as a part of your congregation's stewardship ministry, with the same goal as all of your stewardship ministry—to help people grow in their relationship with Jesus Christ through the use of the financial resources entrusted to them by God. Capital fund appeals present opportunities for people to grow in their response to God's generosity in a way that can last for years after the capital fund appeal has ended.

- ◯ Consider combining a mission project with your capital fund appeal. Many congregations tithe their income from a fund appeal. Ten percent or more is given away to another ministry.

- ◯ Consider a ministry fund appeal. Some congregations have conducted a special appeal for a ministry opportunity, such as adding new staff or adding a new program, such as a preschool. These fund appeals are conducted like capital fund appeals, only it is a ministry opportunity—not a building— that is being funded.

- ◯ Allow people to designate, but don't encourage it. If your capital fund appeal is for several projects, allow people to designate their giving to one project. This will encourage people to give, even if they only support one of the projects. Be careful how you encourage people to designate, though. You don't want to end up with more money for one part of the project than you need for that part. In most congregations the number of people who actually designate is lower than leaders expect.

Endowment funds

Every congregation should have an endowment fund. Most denominations provide assistance to congregations setting up an endowment fund. The funds are not difficult to establish and provide many benefits to congregations.

Endowment funds allow congregations to support ministries they might not otherwise be able to support. How earnings from the endowment fund will be spent are an important part of the documents that establish the endowment fund. Most congregations distribute the earnings both to projects within the congregation and to ministries outside the congregation.

Endowment funds encourage members to remember the congregation in their wills. Since an endowment fund keeps the principal in perpetuity, many people give to a congregation's endowment fund because they know that their gift will continue to provide for the congregation's ministry for as long as the congregation exists.

The existence of an endowment fund provides a way for a congregation to receive a large gift without this gift dividing the congregation. There are horror stories of congregations receiving a gift of several hundred thousand dollars, being totally unprepared for the gift, and then sinking into a huge fight over how the money should be spent. Congregational members are usually very agreeable as they develop a plan for how to receive a large gift before any money is received. Once the money is received, if there is no plan in place, a congregational fight is almost guaranteed.

Giving Begets Giving

Sometimes congregational stewardship leaders are reluctant to offer additional opportunities for people to give through the congregation. The fear is that if people give in a variety of ways, this will reduce the amount people give through the regular offering of the congregation. The experience of the vast majority of congregations is that this simply does not happen.

When God's people have opportunities to give, giving begets giving. Additional giving opportunities create interest in new ministries, create new connections with both the congregation and programs beyond the congregation, and in general strengthen individuals' connections with the church and with the Lord of the church.

We need to go back to the idea with which we began this chapter. The giving pie is not of fixed size. God's people are not an 8-inch pie that cannot get larger. God's people may start as an 8-inch pie (some start much smaller than this), but growth can and does happen. One way to help God's people grow in their giving is to provide them with opportunities to support God's work in a variety of ways. The regular support of the congregation will always be the cornerstone of most people's giving. The additional giving opportunities you provide will be the occasion for people to build on that cornerstone, and to grow from an 8-inch pie into a nice, high 10-inch pie.

Summary

The goal of our stewardship ministry is to help God's people grow in their relationship with Jesus through the use of the time, talents, and finances that God has entrusted to them.

Giving opportunities in the congregation beyond the regular Sunday offering can help people grow in their giving, and grow in their relationship with Jesus. Instead of competing with the Sunday offerings, these additional giving opportunities can actually help create a culture of generosity within the congregation. Furthermore, additional giving opportunities provide God's people with an excellent vehicle to connect service with their giving.

As stewardship leaders, you will want to carefully assess the congregation's history of additional giving opportunities. Use this history as a starting point from which people can be invited to give to exciting ministry opportunities that the leaders of the congregation choose to lift up before them.

Chapter 8

Improving How You Ask

In the church we have seldom asked ourselves the question, "Are we using the most effective means as people are asked to give?" Rather, we have usually fallen back on the seven last words of the church, "We've always done it that way before." How we have asked in the past is usually the way we ask in the present.

Studies have been done on the most effective ways to ask people to consider giving to an organization. Your stewardship leadership team can learn from these studies, and improve the way you ask people in your congregation to give.

Effective Ways to Ask

What is the most effective way to ask someone to give? Here is a compilation from several different studies. The following are listed in order, from most effective to least effective.

1. Two people speaking face-to-face with a giver.
2. One person speaking face-to-face with a giver.
3. A personal letter on stationery, with a telephone follow-up.

This letter is written specifically to an individual giver highlighting the giver's history with the organization, and is not a form letter with the giver's name typed at the top.

4. A personal letter on stationery, with no follow-up.

5. A personal telephone call, with a letter follow-up.

6. A personal telephone call, with no follow-up.

7. A form letter with the giver's name typed in at the top.

8. Telephone solicitation in which a group of people gather together and call strangers from a list of potential givers.

9. Impersonal letter that includes something like, "Dear member," as the salutation.

10. An event

This list can be helpful to your stewardship leadership team in a number of ways.

○ *Analyze your past asking.* Of the methods listed, which have you used in the past? How effective have you found them to be?

○ *Decide to move up to a more effective method of asking.* Not surprisingly, the more effective methods are more personal and more labor intensive. The closer you get to number one on the list, the more work will be involved. As in other aspects of life, the harder you work, the more effective your results will be.

○ *Vary your methods of asking.* You won't want to ask the same way every year. Use this list as suggested ways of asking. Remember though, if you take the easy way out and go to a much lower spot on the list, your results may suffer.

Motivations for Giving

Another important piece of research that has been done is to ask people who give to organizations why they have given. What are the top motivators for people who give financial support to a non-profit organization? Here is one list, again in order of importance from most to least.

1. Being asked by someone you know well
2. You volunteer at the organization
3. Being asked by clergy to give
4. Reading or hearing a news story
5. Being asked to give at work
6. Receiving a letter asking you to give
7. Receiving a telephone call asking you to give

There are a number of important insights that your stewardship team can gather from this short list.

○ *Build a strong volunteer base.* Almost all of your congregation's givers will also be involved in some way in the life of the congregation. Some will sing in the choir, some will be a part of the men's or women's organization, some will serve on a committee or council. Most will be regular worshipers. You have the built-in loyalty of those who give to your congregation. They already are active in the programs of the congregation. This is a huge asset.

○ *Make sure your pastor(s) is/are involved in asking people to give.* As I have mentioned earlier, sometimes pastors are reluctant to be actively involved in stewardship ministry, and sometimes the congregation wants the pastor to be on the sidelines in stewardship ministry. Don't let this happen. The pastor preaches, teaches, and talks to the congregation about all sorts of spiritual issues—make sure that stewardship is included along with other important spiritual issues. The pastor needs to be a part of the stewardship leadership team, and the pastor needs to be involved in asking people to consider their financial giving to the congregation.

○ *Tell a compelling stewardship story.* People don't give to their congregation because they read or hear about what the congregation is doing. Knowing what the congregation is doing, however, will help people know that their gifts are making a difference in people's lives. Knowing what the congregation is doing will encourage people to grow in their giving.

○ *Consider the first effective way to ask—being asked by someone you know well—carefully in your planning.* What are ways you can ensure that people are asked to give to your congregation by someone they know well? If you do an every-member visit, or a series of telephone calls, don't just assign visits or calls to people. Let those who will visit or telephone select the people they will contact, encouraging them to select people they know.

○ *Plan for multiple motivators.* Obviously, the more motivators people in your congregation experience, the more they will be motivated to give generously to Christ's work through your congregation.

Focus on the Giver

Regularly ask yourself the most basic stewardship leadership question, "What can we do to help people grow in their relationship with Jesus Christ through their stewardship?" A constant temptation faced by any group of leaders in the congregation is the temptation to focus on what meets the needs of the leaders, rather than what meets the needs of the members of the congregation. Stewardship leaders are not immune to this temptation. It is easy to start thinking about what will work best for the leadership team. Resist this temptation. Focus instead on what will work best for the givers. Here are a few items to consider:

Timing

Timing of stewardship programs, especially the annual stewardship response program, is crucial. Make sure you conduct these programs when you will have the attention of the maximum number of people.

In the part of the country where I live, deer hunting is a ritual that approaches religious devotion for some. Deer hunting season is the first two weekends in November, which also happens to be a very convenient time to do an annual stewardship response program for those congregations who have a calendar fiscal year. It would be very easy for a stewardship leadership team to say, "Early November works best for us. If people really care about the congregation they will be sure to be involved in our program." Why do this? It focuses on the need of the leaders, not the need of the givers.

If you live in a part of the country in which large numbers of givers head south for the winter, or arrive from the north for the winter, take this into account in your timing. Discuss timing among your stewardship leadership team. What makes the most sense in light of the needs of your givers?

Think generationally

In many congregations, the "model giver" is over fifty years of age, highly committed to the church, and understands that giving is his or her duty. Many stewardship leadership teams direct their efforts, either consciously or unconsciously, to this model giver.

Study after study has shown that givers under fifty are very different from those over fifty. Younger generations are not as committed to institutions, and certainly do not understand financial support of an institution to be their duty. Rather, younger generations want to give financial support to those organizations in which they also are able to give of their time and talents. Younger generations are much more inclined to give where they can see their giving making a difference.

Don't assume that all givers are created the same. Talk to younger members of your congregation about their giving. Make sure you have younger people on your stewardship leadership team. Strategize about how to appeal to all givers in your congregation, not just to that model giver.

Electronic giving

For many givers in your congregation, especially younger givers and those who travel frequently, electronic giving can be an appealing and responsible way to practice financial stewardship. Some givers do as many financial transactions as possible through automatic withdrawal. Other givers may be gone from the community for months at a time, yet still want to make a regular gift to their congregation. Automatic withdrawal provides these people with a convenient way to respond to Christ's call to regular giving.

Electronic giving programs will, of course, not appeal to everyone. Often they will only be utilized by a small percentage of the congregation. Never mind. Since they will meet the needs of some givers, your stewardship team should make sure that your congregation has an electronic giving program in place, and that members of the congregation are regularly reminded of its existence.

Be positive

When you ask people to financially support your congregation and its ministries, focus on what will happen when they give, rather than what won't happen if they don't give. This is quite obvious, but sometimes we forget the obvious.

People are motivated to give to organizations that are making a positive difference in the world. People will be motivated to give generously to your congregation when they perceive it to be making a positive difference in the lives of members, in your community, and in God's kingdom around the world. People will not be motivated by appeals to keep this or that program alive by their giving.

Listen to your stewardship team's language. If you are saying things like, "Because of you . . ." and "We will be able to . . ." then you are being positive. On the other hand, if you hear yourself saying things like, "If we don't . . ." or worse, "If you don't . . ." then you have slipped into negative language. Be positive.

Variety is the spice of life

Sameness causes people to grow bored and to tune out. Make sure that your team's work is varied and fresh. Tell your message in different ways, using different media. Make sure that your print materials don't look the same from month to month, and year to year. Have different people from different walks of life give talks in worship. It is certainly easier to pull out last year's materials and tweak them a little bit, but doing this will almost certainly give them a feel of sameness, not freshness.

Sometimes it is impossible for stewardship team members to tell if they are staying fresh and varied. The old saying, "You can't see the forest for the trees," is true. Consult with others in the congregation. Encourage them to be honest.

Summary

The goal of our stewardship ministry is to help God's people grow in their relationship with Jesus through the use of the time, talents, and finances God has entrusted to them.

The focus of this chapter has been on helping your leadership team be more effective as you ask people to grow in their giving. It is important that you do your stewardship work well so that members might clearly hear and respond to Christ's call to faithful stewardship.

Finding effective ways to ask people to give, motivating givers to respond generously to God's generosity, and focusing on the needs of the giver are all ways that you can encourage giving to Christ and Christ's church. Remember, this isn't about getting enough money to simply run the church. Jesus said, "Where your treasure is, there your heart will be also" (Matt. 6:21). Your stewardship work is about encouraging people to place their treasure in the hands of the One who is the source and owner of all things. When they do that, their hearts will follow.

Chapter 9

Thank

WHEN MY WIFE OR I MAKE A GIFT TO A NONPROFIT organization, I am regularly shocked—and pleased—at how quickly we receive a thank-you note from the organization. I recently mailed a check to the seminary I attended. I usually assume that it takes two days for mail to reach the city where the seminary is located and two days for mail to come from that city. I mailed the check on Monday. In my mail on Wednesday came an acknowledgement and a thank-you. I was impressed.

The local congregation can't do same-day thank-yous for every gift received. This would be a very poor use of time, and would be far more than anyone would expect. Most congregations I know, however, should do much more thanking than they do. Thanking should be a part of the culture of every congregation. People who give to support the ministry of their congregation should be thanked regularly. People who are active in the life of the congregation, and the life of the community, should expect to be regularly recognized and thanked for the work they do.

Paul regularly uses his letters as opportunities to thank God for his fellow believers. Romans, Philippians, Colossians,

1 Thessalonians, and Philemon all contain strong statements of thanks to God for Paul's fellow believers and their faith. Philippians 1:3-5 is typical, "I thank my God every time I remember you, constantly praying with joy in every one of my prayers for all of you, because of your sharing in the gospel from the first day until now."

There are two important things to notice in Paul's thanksgiving. First, he seems eager to give thanks. This provides a great model for us. We should be equally eager to give thanks for those with whom we share faith in Jesus Christ. Second, Paul tells people he thanks God for them. Sometimes we need to say thanks directly to people. "Thank you for your work at the community food shelf" is an important thing to say. Sometimes, when we genuinely feel moved to do so, we should thank God in our prayers for the work of specific people. When we do this, and then tell that person that we have thanked God for them in our prayers, we have taken our thanksgiving to a whole new level.

Creating a Culture of Thanksgiving

There are few things that will build up a congregation more than having a culture of thanksgiving. By this I mean a culture in which people feel comfortable and natural expressing their thanks to one another. When people are regularly thanked, they will not only feel appreciated, they will feel valuable, they will feel wanted and needed. When people are thanked and feel appreciated, they will quickly volunteer to be involved in the next project, whether that be through time, talent, or financial support.

There are some specific steps you as stewardship leaders can take to create a culture of thanksgiving in your congregation:

Start with God

Regularly thank God for gifts God has entrusted to the congregation. One important step to acknowledging God as the source and owner of all is to thank God for what you have under your management. You can do this in worship, in prayers, in hymns, in the sermon. You can do this in committee meetings during devotions. When you do this over and over, thanking God will become a way of life, and it will deepen your understanding that God, not you, owns all that you have. It won't happen overnight, but it will happen.

Another way to start with God is to follow Paul's lead and thank God for the ways people in the congregation have lived out their faith and used their gifts. Have a petition each week in the prayers of the church that thanks God for the specific lives and work of one or two people in the congregation. Encourage the pastor and stewardship leaders to thank God for specific people, and then to tell those people that you have lifted them up in prayer.

Plan your thanksgiving

Most of us don't have the gift of spontaneous thanksgiving. I don't, so I am regularly envious of those who do. Thanking people should be a part of the planning for any stewardship program. Before any annual response program is conducted, plan how you will thank not only those who estimate their giving, but also those who lead the program. If you do mission of the month, make sure that someone has the responsibility to thank those who provide leadership each month. Whatever your leadership team does, remember to plan to give thanks. This is a sure way to make sure thanks is given.

Expand the circle of thanks-givers

It is important that the pastor takes leadership in giving thanks. For most people, a thank you from the pastor is very meaningful. But the pastor can't—and shouldn't—be the only thanks-giver. Find those people in your congregation who do have the gift of thanksgiving, and turn them loose with your blessing. Give them a pile of thank-you notes, envelopes, and stamps, and encourage them to use them up and come back for more. Make sure that stewardship leaders and other leaders in the congregation are encouraged to give thanks, both written and verbal.

Thank everyone at the same time

There will be many times during the course of a year that thank-yous extended to large groups of people are appropriate and important. At the end of the annual stewardship program you will want to thank the entire congregation in worship as you announce the results of the program. When other large congregation-wide projects have been completed, say thanks to everyone as you describe what has been accomplished. Again, make sure that different people extend these thank-yous. Your thanks will be more personal as different people who have been involved with different programs stand in worship to offer their appreciation.

Thank personally

Along with thanking everyone at the same time, make sure your congregation is characterized by personal thank-yous as well. These thank-yous can be extended in a brief note from the pastor or a congregational leader. Or these thank-yous can be extended face to face. How they are delivered isn't nearly as important as that they are delivered. It is safe to say you can't thank too often. Too seldom, yes, but never too often. If leaders set the example of personal thanks, it is possible that, pretty soon after the example is set, thank-yous will be flying all over the congregation.

Thank immediately

As I described at the beginning of this chapter, immediate thanksgiving truly expresses strong appreciation. With apologies to those who are procrastinators, it is true that the sooner a thank-you is received, the more sincere it will be perceived. This is why planning to thank is so important. You are much more likely to thank quickly when you have planned to thank.

I know a pastor who sets aside a few minutes every Monday morning for thank-you note writing. He writes any worship assistants from Sunday morning, he writes anyone who shared musical talents, he sometimes writes an usher or two, occasionally he will write a quick note to a worshiper he didn't get a chance to speak with after worship. None of this takes much time, but its impact on the life of the congregation is profound.

Pass on thank-yous
From time to time your congregation will receive thank-yous from other ministries you support. It is important that stewardship leaders understand that these thank-yous are not written to the pastor or to the stewardship leadership team—they are written to the entire congregation. Pass these thank-yous on. If they are very brief, perhaps they could be read in worship. They could be included in the newsletter or as in insert in the Sunday bulletin. At the very least, they could be posted on a bulletin board. Make sure that expressions of thanks to the congregation are heard by the congregation.

Hold thank-you trips
If you support a ministry that is within a few hours drive of your congregation, consider conducting a "thank-you trip" to visit that ministry. You will probably want to invite anyone in the congregation who would like to go, but make sure you extend a special invitation to those who have particular interest in this ministry, or who have been key leaders in the congregation's support of the ministry. Perhaps you could take a check that embodies your financial support of the ministry.

Holding such a trip is a win-win situation. People who have worked hard for the ministry will know that their work is valued by the congregation's leadership. And then, when they see the ministry, they will not only hear appreciation from leaders of that ministry, they will also see the good work that is being done because of your congregation's financial support.

These are a few suggestions of ways you can start to create a climate of thanksgiving in your congregation. Obviously, this is not an exhaustive list. Spend some time with your stewardship leadership team talking about these suggestions, then turn your imaginations loose. What are some other ways of thanking that have worked or would work well in your congregation?

Some Great Opportunities to Say "Thanks"

There are some times during the course of the year when stewardship leaders have opportunities to say thanks that should not be missed. Again, the list that follows is intended to be suggestive, not exhaustive. You will want to create your own list that fits your congregation.

After receiving an estimate of giving card

Have a system in place so that you respond to each estimate of giving card immediately upon receipt of the card. Don't wait until all cards are received. In some cases, this can occur over several weeks. The thank-you letter should come either from the pastor or from one of the stewardship leaders. In addition to thanking the person who has submitted the estimate of giving card, the letter should also give the specific amount of the estimate. This provides an opportunity to make sure that the amount recorded matches the giver's intent.

In addition to saying thanks and giving the amount of the estimate, this letter can also serve as a way to give thanks to God for what the congregation has accomplished in the past year, and to ask for God's guidance as you meet the opportunities of the coming year. An excellent format for this letter might be a paragraph describing some highlights of the past year, a paragraph looking forward to opportunities in the coming year, and a paragraph thanking the giver for their financial support of the congregation, their estimate for the coming year, and a listing of the specific amount of that estimate.

Each quarter along with the record of giving

Many congregations mail out a quarterly record of giving to members. This mailing should include a thank-you letter. Merely putting a one-sentence thank you at the bottom of the record of giving is a missed opportunity. Include a letter that thanks the givers for their support. In this letter highlight one or two ministries of the congregation. Let people know how their support of the congregation is making a difference in someone's life.

Every gift that is mailed to the church

I know a pastor who writes a thank-you note to everyone who mails their regular offering to the church. If givers are gone for a couple months, he asks how they are doing, and includes a little news from home. If the people are seldom in worship, he offers words of encouragement to become a part of the worshiping community. He claims this task takes only minutes each week.

Any extra gift that is mailed to the church should be treated in the same way a gift to any non-profit organization is treated. A system should be in place so a prompt thank-you is sent. Examples of such gifts would be memorial gifts, gifts to special program or building funds, and so on.

Acknowledgement of community recognition

When a member of the congregation is recognized in the community newspaper, many congregations post the newspaper article on a bulletin board. This is great. It would also be great if someone volunteered to write a short note from the church acknowledging that person's accomplishment and thanking them from the congregation. You could have thank-you notes printed with the church's picture or a special logo, provide the volunteer with a roll of stamps, and turn them loose.

Thanks to volunteers

Find another volunteer to keep his or her eyes open for people in the congregation who have volunteered in one way or another. Ask the volunteer to recognize a Sunday school teacher, a musician, a volunteer at a Habitat for Humanity project—the list of possibilities is endless. Use the same thank-you notes described above, and have someone write a few notes per week to volunteers.

Personal thank-you notes from the pastor
Even the busiest pastor could find twenty minutes each week to write five short thank-you notes to people who come to mind. These could be people who have made a special contribution of time, talent, or finances, or people who are having a special birthday or anniversary, or people who just come to the pastor's mind as someone they appreciate. A personal note from the pastor asking for nothing, just saying thanks, would brighten anyone's day.

Summary

The goal of our stewardship ministry is to help God's people grow in their relationship with Jesus through the use of the time, talents, and finances God has entrusted to them.

Say thanks. Create a culture of thanksgiving in your congregation by being stewardship leaders who model giving thanks often. Let the Apostle Paul encourage you as you consider how eager he was to thank God for his brothers and sisters in Christ.

Take some time as stewardship leaders to plan how you will give thanks. Expand the circle of thanks-givers by involving and empowering others in giving thanks. Look for opportunities to give thanks, and then seize those opportunities quickly. For better or for worse, the moment to say thanks most effectively is a fleeting moment.

Plan also to say thanks at specific, important moments. Find people with the spiritual gift of thanksgiving, and involve them in the ministry of your stewardship leadership team. Develop materials that they can use to extend the congregation's thanks.

Give thanks to members for their work. Give thanks to God for the members' faithful service. Giving thanks is as important to stewardship work as asking. Plan to say thanks with as much care as you plan to ask.

Chapter 10

Tell

GOD'S PEOPLE WANT TO KNOW THAT THEIR GIVING MAKES A difference in people's lives. This simple truth forms the basis for the third key word in your stewardship ministry—tell. It's not just that people want to know that their giving makes a difference—they deserve to know that their giving makes a difference. No one should give to your congregation and feel that his or her gift has fallen into a black hole. Each giver deserves the joy of knowing that God's work has been done because of his or her giving.

There is an important connection between thanking, which we talked about in the last chapter, and telling, which is the topic of this chapter. That important connection is that you can tell as you thank, and you can thank as you tell. In fact, much of your telling can occur in the context of thanking people for their giving, and in almost all of your thanking, telling will be an important part of the thanking. To be sure, there will be times when you will simply tell the story of your ministry for the sake of telling, without a word of thanks. There will also be times when you will miss a great opportunity if you don't tell in the context of thanking.

I have long operated with the principle that in the church you need to say something seven times in seven different ways before you can expect that people have heard your message. Recently I heard a marketer say that you shouldn't expect a response from someone until they have heard your message eleven times. I don't know if the magic number is seven or eleven, or somewhere in between. I do know that as you tell people in your congregation about the ministry of your congregation, you can't assume that telling a time or two using only one medium will get the job done. As stewardship leaders, you will need to be creative and persistent as you tell people what happens through your congregation because of their giving.

The Importance of Telling Your Mission Story

Why should you have to tell your congregation's mission story? Shouldn't people give simply in response to God's generosity? Of course they should, and they probably do. The point of telling isn't so much to encourage people to give as it is to encourage people to give to your congregation.

We all have countless opportunities to give. Many worthwhile organizations fill our mailboxes with requests for our dollars. Your congregation isn't the only fish in the giving sea. It is important to tell your mission story so that members of your congregation know how their giving to the congregation makes a difference. It is also important to tell your mission story to motivate people to give generously to your congregation.

Fund-raisers talk about an organization "making a case," that is, establishing that the organization is a worthwhile recipient of people's gifts. As a congregation, you don't have to make a case in quite the same way. Members of your congregation have already joined the congregation. They shouldn't need convincing that the congregation is a worthwhile organization. However, they do need to know that good things are happening because of their giving. If they don't know this, you have provided them no reason to increase their giving to the church rather than increasing their gift to some other worthwhile organization.

Telling is important. Telling motivates people to give more generously to your congregation.

How to Tell Your Mission Story

As I indicated above, your telling needs to be both frequent and varied. Saying something one time in a worship announcement is certainly better than saying nothing at all. But you can't expect your message to be communicated with this one telling.

Our telling needs to be frequent because we live in a society in which we are bombarded by messages. Some studies have indicated that we are receiving thousands of marketing messages every day. Because of this, we have unintentionally become quite adept at tuning things out. We are sort of like kids who have the amazing ability to not hear what their parents say, especially when they don't like the message. You simply must repeat your message in order to break through this "tuning out."

Our telling needs to be varied because in even the smallest congregation every person is more responsive to some communication media, and less responsive to others. If you are going to reach as many people as possible with your message, you need to tell it in as many different ways as you can imagine.

The congregation's newsletter

Most congregations have newsletters. These newsletters provide an opportunity to tell your story to the whole congregation, even those seldom in worship. The problem with newsletters is that you have no guarantee that anyone reads them. My own experience in ministry is that the more a person is in worship, the more likely they are to read the newsletter. The exception to this is shut-ins, for whom the newsletter is a regular link to a congregation they love, and therefore, they will often read it from cover to cover.

Newsletter articles should be short and to the point. Make sure they begin with a sentence that captures the reader's interest, or the reader may not get past the first sentence. If you highlight a ministry of the congregation in the same place in each monthly newsletter, readers may develop the habit of looking for this article.

E-mails to members

More and more congregations send regular e-mails to all members who make their e-mail address available to the congregation. We all hate to be drowned in e-mails, so be careful you don't abuse the privilege of having access to people's e-mail addresses. On the other hand, an occasional e-mail telling of a ministry of the congregation should make more interesting reading than many of the e-mails we may get. Again, short and to the point is good. E-mails might also be a good place to combine telling with a word of thanks for supporting the ministry described.

Your congregation's Web site

Again, more and more congregations are developing their own Web sites. Occasionally highlighting a ministry of the congregation on the front page of the Web site provides members with the opportunity to learn more. Combining information on the Web site with an e-mail to members telling them to go to the Web site for more information accomplishes two goals: it gets the information out, and it gets people to visit the congregation's Web site.

The congregation's Web site also provides an easy link to the Web sites of other ministries that your congregation supports. Your national church, a Bible camp you support, a college of your church—these and many more ministries you support have their own Web sites. Linking to them is easy.

A stewardship bulletin board

Every congregation should have a stewardship bulletin board. Hopefully this stewardship bulletin board can be in a high-traffic location in your congregation's building. Every month this bulletin board could be changed to tell the story of a different ministry of the congregation. If you simply want to tell a mission story—do it here. If you want people to sign up to support a ministry—do it here. Get people used to going to the stewardship bulletin board for ministry news.

A word of suggestion: Your congregation has two or three artistically talented people. If they are in a profession that uses bulletin boards, like elementary school teachers, all the better. Turn these two or three people loose on the stewardship bulletin board.

Talks in worship

Talks in worship can be effective ways to tell your congregation's ministry stories, especially if the person giving the talk has a personal connection to the specific ministry he or she is describing. Like newsletter articles, these talks should be short and to the point. This is no time for impromptu speeches. Rambling is deadly. Keep facts and figures to a minimum. Stories about how people's lives have been changed are key to an interesting and effective talk.

Bulletin inserts

Many people get to church a little early. Perhaps this is because they know that late arrivers might end up sitting in one of the front pews. At any rate, bulletin inserts can provide some reading material for those who are early. Also, more than a few bulletins get put in purses or coat pockets, so those inserts might be read later at home.

The wonderful thing about bulletin inserts is that many of the ministries your congregation supports will provide you with all the inserts you need. If you want to highlight a local ministry and need to create your own insert, they are easy to produce. Again, find someone in the congregation with good desktop publishing skills and let them work their magic.

Adult education classes

An excellent way to do a much more detailed presentation on a ministry of the congregation or a ministry that the congregation supports is to use adult education time on Sunday morning. Many congregations have such a time available, and many ministries have video presentations that describe the work they do. Often, representatives of ministries are available to come to your congregation and lead an adult class. If a representative comes to your congregation, make sure to give him or her the opportunity to give a short talk in worship—there are usually more people in worship than in the adult class.

A mission fair

A mission fair is a way to tell the whole story of your congregation's ministry in one grand display. A mission fair takes quite a bit of work, but is worth the effort. Gather information from as many of your congregation's ministries as you can, and make displays of all the ways your congregation is making a difference in people's lives. Invite representatives of ministries you support to bring a display. Turn your fellowship hall or other large meeting area into a place where people can see and talk about all that you are doing. Tell what you are doing in your own community, and what you are doing through others that you support across the country and around the world.

As stewardship leaders, you know your congregation better than anyone else does. Are there other ways of telling your story that I haven't mentioned here? It is safe to say that there is no wrong way to communicate the story of your congregation's ministry. Be as creative as you can be.

Before leaving this section on how to tell the story, let me also remind you of opportunities, such as mission of the month, sponsorships, and seasonal appeals that were discussed in chapter 7. Each of these provide not only an opportunity to ask people to support a specific ministry, they also provide a great opportunity to tell the story of the ministry. Some of the very best talks in worship I have ever heard have been people telling about a specific mission of the month in the congregation in which I am a member. These talks are almost always personal and compelling. Again, seize every opportunity to tell your story.

Getting the Information You Need to Tell the Story

We live in the information age. Some would claim that we are inundated with information. The challenge you will face in telling your story will not be gathering enough information, but rather sorting through the available information to find the most helpful information.

Mail received by your congregation will continue to be a primary source of information for stewardship leaders. Often stewardship leaders face a challenge in getting this information directed to them. An important first step in receiving information through the mail is to find out how mail is handled when it arrives at your congregation. Is there a church secretary who distributes the mail? Does the pastor receive all the mail? Whoever this key person is, make sure you communicate with them how important it is for you to see mail that arrives from ministries you support. Perhaps the stewardship team can have a mail box set aside for you.

The Internet is another great source for information. It is likely that every ministry your congregation supports has a Web site. As a stewardship leader, you should regularly visit those sites. The Web site itself will be a great source of information. Also, the Web site will let you know how to request other material, such as print material that you can use on the stewardship bulletin board or for a mission fair.

Your own members are also a great source for information. Your congregation's members obviously know more about each individual ministry of your congregation than anyone else. You also have members who have connections with many of the ministries you support. Utilize these members. Asking them for help will affirm their involvement in the ministry of the congregation.

Don't forget your regional and national church structures as great sources of information. Most churches have middle judicatories—which is a twenty-five-cent name for what are often called synods, districts, presbyteries, and so on. These middle judicatories are supported by congregations, and in turn often support many statewide ministries. Your congregation's support of a state council of churches, a Bible camp, a college, or a seminary may well happen through the middle judicatory. Your middle judicatory's Web site will probably be a great source of information about these ministries that you support.

Your national church structure is your link to ministry around the world. Through your national church, your congregation is doing exciting work in Jesus' name that will surprise and delight you. You are probably supporting missionaries, starting new congregations, fighting hunger, and much, much more. In too many congregations these wonderful stories of ministry go untold, causing people to feel no connection with the church of which they are a part. Again, the Internet is a great starting place. Many national church structures also produce wonderful print pieces that tell their story. My denomination, the ELCA, has an annual publication in a news magazine format that does a great job of telling stories of ministry.

With a little effort, you will find that your stewardship leadership team has all the information it needs to tell the story of your congregation's ministry to its members. Just as you need to employ different media as you tell your story, you will want to explore different media to get the information you need.

A Few Other Tips for Telling Your Story

Think local–national–global
As you tell your story, strive for a balance among local ministry, regional and national ministry, and global ministry. You might want to be very intentional about planning a schedule of monthly emphases that rotates among these. Focusing too much on only one of these three will weaken the story that you have to tell.

Do everything you can to be interesting
As I have indicated above, most people don't find numbers interesting. Most people do find human interest stories compelling. People want to hear about people. If your congregation or community has a connection with a far-away ministry, make sure you emphasize that connection. If you are talking about a ministry in your community and confidentiality concerns don't prohibit it, make sure you talk about people in your congregation who are involved in that ministry.

Connect the story to the expected response
If you are asking people to financially support a ministry you are describing, make sure you say that clearly. Also, be very clear about how people can make a financial contribution. Don't make the mistake of getting people excited about a ministry and then making them wait two weeks before giving them the opportunity to make a gift. Excitement can fade quite dramatically in two weeks.

Summary

The goal of our stewardship ministry is to help God's people grow in their relationship with Jesus through the use of the time, talents, and finances God has entrusted to them.

Effectively telling the story of your congregation's ministry and the story of the ministries your congregation supports will help God's people grow in their relationship with Jesus. As people know that they are making a difference in other people's lives, they will be drawn closer to their brothers and sisters in Christ, and they will be motivated to grow in their generosity.

As you tell your story, it is important that you tell it often, and in varied ways. If you want to reach as many people as possible, you simply must tell the same story over and over again in a variety of ways. God has provided you with a vast array of ways to tell your congregation's story—use them all.

You also have countless ways to gather information for this telling. The mail is a great source of information, but don't just sit around waiting for information to drop into your hands courtesy of the postal service. Use the Internet, use people in your congregation, use any resources at your disposal to gather information. Maybe your stewardship leadership team should have as one of its members someone who has a little detective in their personality.

The previous chapter talked about thanking. This chapter talks about telling. I want to end this chapter by again pointing out that these two—thanking and telling—can often be linked. I also want to say that, like thanking, telling is an activity that isn't ever finished. There is always another ministry story to tell. Thanks be to God for that.

Chapter 11

Organizing for Your Stewardship Ministry

By now, I hope you are saying to yourself, "Wow, our stewardship committee is never going to be able to do all of this." I hope you are saying this, because it is true. I've never worked with a stewardship committee that could effectively respond to the call to ask, thank, and tell that has been issued in the previous chapters. It is important that you recognize this, because if you try to embark on a stewardship ministry as thorough as has been described here, and if you try to do that with the standard stewardship committee, you are doomed to failure.

How can you effectively carry out the stewardship ministry that has been described in the preceding chapters? I want to suggest to you an organizational structure that is built around work groups made up of people selected because of the gifts God has given them. You can still have a stewardship committee if you must, but the work will get done by the work groups, not in a committee meeting.

Three Work Groups

My suggestion is that you form three work groups—one around each of the three main stewardship tasks that I have put forth here. You will have one work group responsible for planning and implementing the various ways you will ask those in the congregation to give of the time, talents, and financial resources that God has entrusted to them. You will have one work group charged to cultivate the climate of thanksgiving in your congregation. The third work group will be about telling everyone in the congregation about the wonderful ministry that is happening in the congregation and around the world because of their giving.

Depending on the size of your congregation, these work groups could be as small as two people or as large as ten. It all depends on how much asking, thanking, and telling you will do. These work groups can be larger or smaller as tasks come and go.

How Should These Work Groups Function?

Each work group will be made up of people who have been identified, recruited, and empowered because they have the gifts needed to carry out the task of their specific group. Don't limit yourself to people who are already on the stewardship committee. They may or may not be the right people for these work groups.

First, think about the spiritual gifts needed for each group. Someone on each group will need the gift of organization. For the asking group, you will want people who are comfortable talking about money to a group of people, and people who have demonstrated the gift of generous giving in their own lives. For the thanking group, you will want people who have a spirit of thanksgiving and who can cultivate that gift in others. For the telling group, you will need people with good communication skills, both speaking and writing. Each group can add new people as new ideas come along that need to be developed and implemented.

Second, recruit people to serve on the specific work group that will utilize their gifts. Tell people why they are being asked to serve on that specific group. Don't get a bunch of people together and say, "Now, who wants to be on which group?" Some of the most ineffective congregational structures I have seen are caused by people being elected to the church council, and then at the first meeting someone asks the question, "Who wants to work on which committee?" Don't make that same mistake in your stewardship ministry. Ask people to serve on the specific work group that needs their unique gifts.

Third, empower these groups. Turn them loose. Don't let your congregation council or a stewardship committee be permission-givers, who must review every idea and decide whether or not it will happen. That is deadly. Make sure each group has the authority to dream and act in their area of responsibility without having to get permission from anyone. If you can't trust the members of the work group, you have the wrong people on the work group.

Fourth, make sure these work groups are work groups. Don't gather the work groups monthly for meetings. Most people today are running as fast as they can from additional meetings. Let the work groups work. Gather the work groups together only often enough to make sure that the big picture goals are still in place, and to talk about what other big picture goals ought to be in place. When you are working on a specific project, such as the annual response program, those working on that project will obviously need to meet often enough to plan and conduct the program. But in all cases your goal should be fewer meetings, and shorter meetings. Do the work. Don't just talk about the work.

Fifth, in larger congregations, each work group might actually be made up of smaller groups that are working on a specific task. For example, the ask work group might have one smaller group working only on mission of the month, and another working only on the annual response program. The thank work group might have one smaller group writing thank-you notes to members and another making sure that thank-you notes from other ministries get to members of the congregation. The tell work group may have one group working on a stewardship bulletin board and another writing a regular newsletter article.

Sixth, I would modestly suggest that the reading and discussion of this book would be a great place for each work group to start. Don't just have each group look at the chapters that pertain directly to their work. The whole book should be read, discussed, and understood. Then, each group could go back to the chapters that pertain to their work, and use that material as the starting point for planning how they will ask, thank, or tell in your congregation.

What If We Have a Stewardship Committee?

Your congregation's bylaws may require you to have a stewardship committee. If so, don't violate the constitution. Rather, keep the stewardship committee, and make sure it is made up of a least one representative of each work group. This stewardship committee could function as the steering committee for your congregation's stewardship ministry. This steering committee could coordinate the work of all three work groups. This steering committee could make decisions that transcend the work of any one work group. You probably need such a steering committee even if you don't have a formal stewardship committee.

I would add one word of caution. Don't ask this stewardship committee or steering committee to meet monthly. Remember, fewer meetings and shorter meetings are preferred. A quarterly meeting with a carefully planned agenda distributed ahead of time to committee members should allow for more than adequate coordinating and planning.

This stewardship/steering committee might be the place where decisions are made about what annual response program will be used in the coming year; it might be the place where mission of the month partners would be selected; it would certainly be the place where coordination among the three stewardship work groups would happen, so that all groups are working toward the same goals.

Make a Year-Long Plan

As I started to write this chapter, my plan was to suggest a monthly to-do list for each work group, and for the stewardship/steering committee. That plan didn't work. It didn't work because I don't know what each work group in your congregation is going to decide to do, and I'm not at all sure how your stewardship/steering committee will function.

Because of this, I unable to give you a monthly to-do list, but I can say that I think one will be invaluable in your work. Each work group should decide what tasks it will accomplish in the coming year, and then break down each task into a to-do list. Assign each element of that to-do list to a month, and you will have your year-long plan. If this sounds a little too organized, let me assure you that it isn't. This year-long detailed plan is the best way to make sure that items aren't forgotten or only half-completed.

After each work group has a year-long detailed plan, these can be shared and reviewed through the stewardship/steering committee to make sure that the plans fit together and complement each other. Remember, the committee isn't approving the plans. Each work group has the power to develop and implement their own plan. The committee is coordinating for the good of all three work groups.

A Vision of Stewardship Ministry

I don't want to end with all this detail. I want to end by going back to the beginning and saying once more that the goal of stewardship ministry is to help God's people grow in their relationship with Jesus through the use of the time, talents, and finances God has entrusted to them. As I have said many times—it is about discipleship. It is about people's relationship with their Lord. Responsible stewardship will draw people closer to Jesus.

One of my favorite novels is *A Christmas Carol* by Charles Dickens. Each year at Christmas I try to see either a play or movie version of *A Christmas Carol,* or to read the original. A big part of the appeal of *A Christmas Carol* to me is the incredible contrast between Ebenezer Scrooge at the beginning of the story and Ebenezer Scrooge at the end of the story.

Notice Dickens' description of Scrooge from the first pages of his novel, "Oh! But he was a tight-fisted hand at the grindstone, Scrooge! A squeezing, wrenching, grasping, scraping, clutching, covetous old sinner! Hard and sharp as flint, from which no steel had ever struck out generous fire, secret, and self-contained, and solitary as an oyster" (New American Library, 1984, p. 31).

Many, many pages, and three Christmas ghosts later, Scrooge wakes up on Christmas morning. To say the least, he is a changed man. He remembers a huge turkey he has seen in a poultry shop. "'I'll send it to Bob Cratchit's,' whispered Scrooge, rubbing his hands, and splitting with a laugh. 'He shan't know who sends it. It's twice the size of Tiny Tim'" (p. 133).

Send it he does. In fact, the turkey is so large that he says to the delivery boy, "You must have a cab." And then Dickens writes, "The chuckle with which he said this, and the chuckle with which he paid for the cab, and the chuckle with which he recompensed the boy, were only to be exceeded by the chuckle with which he sat down breathless in his chair again, and chuckled till he cried" (p. 133).

I don't wish for any of God's children to be scared to their senses by night visits from past, present, or future ghosts. But I do have a vision of people in your congregation so enjoying their generous giving that they chuckle until they cry. I do have a vision of people in your congregation who discover the radical truth of Jesus' words, "Where your treasure is, there your heart will be also" (Matt. 6:21). I do have a vision of people in your congregation whose generosity grows by leaps and bounds, and who discover that this generosity has indeed led their heart to Jesus. I do have a vision of people chuckling, or at least smiling, as they drop their offering into the plate on Sunday morning.

I do have this vision. I invite you into this same vision.